Exploring Music 4

Eunice Boardman / Beth Landis

illustrated by Walter Brooks

Consultants

Milton Babbitt
Keith E. Baird
Louis W. Ballard
Chou Wen-chung

Dorothy K. Gillett
Alan Lomax
Kurt Miller
Elena Paz

Virginia Stroh Red
Fela Sowande
Kurt Stone
Nelmathilda Woodward

Music autography by Maxwell Weaner

HOLT, RINEHART AND WINSTON, INC.   New York, Toronto, London, Sydney

ISBN: 0-03-084752-4

234567890   032   98765432

Acknowledgments

Grateful acknowledgment is given to the following authors and publishers.

American Ethical Union for "Brethren in Peace Together," and "We Sing of Golden Mornings," adaptation of the text by Vincent Silliman, both from *We Sing of Life*, copyright © 1955 by the American Ethical Union. Used by permission.

The American Museum of Natural History for "A Prayer" from *Anthropological Papers of the American Museum of Natural History*, Vol. 29, page 286, copyright 1928 by the American Museum of Natural History. Used by permission.

Appleseed Music, Inc. for "Pretty Little Girl, Can You Answer Me?" by Ruth Rubin, copyright © 1964 by Appleseed Music, Inc., and "The Power and Glory" by Phil Ochs, Copyright © 1963 and © 1964 by Appleseed Music, Inc. Used by permission.

Atheneum Publishers, Inc. for "Some Uses for Poetry" from *It Doesn't Always Have To Rhyme* by Eve Merriam, copyright © 1964 by Eve Merriam. Used by permission.

Louis Ballard for "Athapascan Indian Bear-Raven Song," and "Quapaw Indian Face-Dance Song". © Copyright 1971 by Louis Ballard. Used by permission.

Mrs. Dorothy M. W. Bean for the words to "All Beautiful the March of Days." Used by permission.

Bowmar Records, Inc. for "Tafta Hindy" from *Folk Songs of the Arab World* by Sally Monsour, copyright © 1969 by Bowmar Records, Inc.

Broadman Press for "Psalm 100" by Jane M. Marshall, copyright © 1960 by Broadman Press.
All rights reserved. International copyright secured. Used by permission.

Cooperative Recreation Service, Inc. for "The Happy Plowman," copyright 1953 by Cooperative Recreation Service, Inc., "Lullaby Round" from *101 Rounds* and "Sim Sala Bim" from *African Songs*, copyright © 1958 by Cooperative Recreation Service, Inc. Used by permission.

Danish American Young People's League for "Hiking, Laughing, Singing," and "Cherries So Ripe." Used by permission.

The John Day Company, Inc. for "Bluebird" and "Frogs" from *Folk Songs of China, Japan, Korea* by Betty Warner Dietz and Thomas Choonbai Park, copyright © 1964 by The John Day Company, Inc. Publisher; "Little Monk," from *The Flower Drum and other Chinese Songs* by Chin-Hsin Yao Chen and Shih-Hsiang Chen, copyright 1943 by Chin-Hsin Yao Chen and Shih-Hsiang Chen. Used by permission.

Friendship Press for "Congo Lullaby" from *The Whole World Singing* by Edith Lovell Thomas. Used by permission.

H. W. Gray Company for "The Yodlers' Carol" by Mary E. Caldwell, copyright © 1964 by H. W. Gray Company. Used by permission.

Gulf Music Company for "America for Me," copyright © 1966 by Gulf Music Company. Used by permission.

Harcourt Brace Jovanovich, Inc. for "Lines Written for Gene Kelly to Dance to" by Carl Sandburg, copyright © 1960 by Carl Sandburg. Reprinted from his volume *Wind Song*; for "Good Advice" from *Rainbow In The Sky*, adapted from the German by Louis Untermeyer, edited by Louis Untermeyer, copyright 1935 by Harcourt Brace Jovanovich, Inc. renewed © 1963 by Louis Untermeyer. Used by permission.

Hokuseido Press, Tokyo, and Hallmark Cards, Inc. for "Verse by Taigi" from *Haiku*, Vol. 2, translated by R. H. Blyth, copyrighted by Hallmark Cards, Inc. Used by permission.

Indian Council for Cultural Relations for "Sleep Brings Pearl Necklaces, Do Not Cry Baby," from *Folk Songs of India*, edited by Hom Barua and published by the Indian Council for Cultural Relations. Reprinted by permission of the editor, Hom Barua.

Indiana University Press for "Forsythia" from *Concrete Poetry: A World View*, edited by Mary Ellen Solt, copyright © 1968 by Hispanic Arts, Indiana University. Used by permission.

Information Canada for "My Arms, They Wave High In The Air," from *Eskimo Songs Vol. 14, Songs of the Copper Eskimos*, by Helen H. Roberts and D. Jenness (Southern party 1913-16) Department of Northern Affairs and National Resources, Ottawa 1925. Used by permission.

Dick James Music, Inc. for "Yellow Submarine" by Lennon-McCartney, copyright © 1966 by Northern Songs Limited. All rights reserved. Used by permission.

Music Sales Corporation for "Rice Harvesting Song" arranged by Venona Johnson, translated by Eleanor Chroman, from *Songs That Children Sing* by Eleanor Chroman, copyright © 1969 by Oak Publications, a division of Embassy Music Corporation. Used by permission.

Oxford University Press for "Banana Boat Loader's Song" from *Folk Songs of Jamaica*, copyright 1952 by Oxford University Press. Used by permission.

Elena Paz for "Arruru." © Copyright 1971 by Elena Paz. Used by permission.

Peter Pauper Press, Inc. for "The Moon Always Follows the Sun," from *African Poems and Love Songs*, copyright © 1970 by Peter Pauper Press, Inc. Used by permission.

Clarkson N. Potter, Inc. for the English words to "Mister Urian," translation by Ronald Duncan, and "The Butterfly," translation by Iris Rogers from *Classical Songs for Children* by the Countess of Harewood and Ronald Duncan, copyright © 1965 by the authors. Used by permission.

Theodore Presser Company for the musical quotations from the *Hary Janos Suite* by Zoltán Kodály, copyright 1927 by Universal Edition, copyright assigned 1952 to Universal Edition (London) Ltd., copyright © renewed 1955. Used by permission of Theodore Presser Company, agents for Universal Edition.

Picture Sources

Contents

The Three Musicians
by Pablo Picasso

Let's Explore Music

We often think of explorers as people who search for new lands. Explorers can also be people who search for new ways to express their feelings and ideas.

Some explorers have discovered new ways of expressing their ideas through creating, performing, or listening to music.

Others have explored new ways of expressing ideas and feelings by dancing, writing a poem, painting a picture, or creating a sculpture.

As you explore music and other arts in this book, you will discover that you can learn to understand and enjoy the ideas of others.

You will also discover new ways to express your own ideas through music and other arts.

The Power and Glory

Words and Music by Phil Ochs

1. C'-mon and take a walk with me
(2.) Col - o - ra - do, Kan-sas,

through this green and grow-in' land,
and the Car - o - li - nas, too, Vir -

Walk through the mead-ows and the moun-tains and the sand,
gin - ia and A - las - ka, from the old___ to the new,

Walk through the val - leys and the riv - ers and the plains,
Tex - as and O - hi - o and the Cal - i - for - nia shore,

Walk through the sun and walk through the rain.
Tell me, who could ask for more?

Here's a land full of pow-er and glo - ry,

Beau - ty that words can-not re - call. ____

Oh, her pow- er shall rest on the strength of her free-dom,

1. Her glo - ry shall rest on us all. ____ 2. From

2. all, ____ on us all. ____

When might people sing this song?

What kinds of feelings or ideas are expressed?

Discuss these questions as you learn other songs.

Begin to make a list of the ways people use music in their lives.

Was the music created to accompany some activity or event such as work, play, or worship?

Was it composed to express feelings such as one's pride in his country, or love of his family?

Add to the list as you learn new music.

Study the other arts to see if similar feelings and ideas are expressed.

Rocka My Soul

Spiritual

Oh, a rock- a my soul __ in the bos-om of A - bra- ham,

A rock- a my soul __ in the bos-om of A - bra- ham,

A rock- a my soul __ in the bos-om of A - bra- ham,

Oh, rock- a my soul.

So high, you can't get o - ver it;

So low, you can't get un- der it;

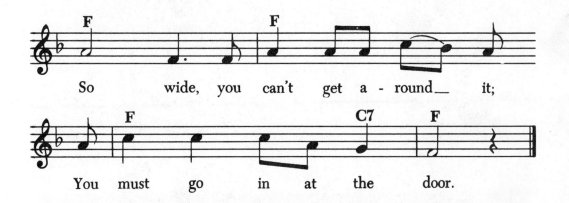

So wide, you can't get a - round__ it;

You must go in at the door.

Polly Wolly Doodle

American Folk Song

Long ago, people often danced as they sang this song.
When you know the melody, plan a dance which matches the design
of the music.

1. Oh, I went down South to see my Sal,
2. Oh, my Sal - ly is a maid - en fair,
3. Be - hind the barn, down on my knees,
4. He ___ sneezed so hard with whoop - ing cough,

Sing Pol - ly wol - ly doo - dle all the day;

My ___ Sal - ly is a spunk - y gal,
With ___ curl - y eyes and laugh - ing hair,
I ___ thought I heard a chick - en sneeze,
He ___ sneezed his head and tail right off,

Sing Pol - ly wol - ly doo - dle all the day.

Refrain

Fare thee well, fare thee well, Fare thee
well, my fair - y fay, For I'm
going to Loui - si - an - a, for to see my Su - sy - an - na,
Sing Pol - ly wol - ly doo - dle all the day.

Divide into three groups. Perform these patterns.

Group 1
(slide palms together)

Group 2 (clap hands)

Group 3 (tap fingertips)

The ♩ will sound with the beat.
Which notes will sound **twice as long** as the ♩ ?
Which notes will sound **half as long** as the ♩ ?

Three different notes are used: **eighth notes, quarter notes,**
and **half notes.** Can you match each note with its name?

Old Texas

Cowboy Song

People often sing as they work. Sometimes they sing songs with a strong rhythm to make their work easier. Sometimes they sing songs which express feelings about their work. For which reason did the cowboy sing this song?

I'm goin' to leave ____ old ___ Tex - as now, ____
They've got no use ____ for the long- horn cow. ____

2. They've plowed and fenced my cattle range,
   And the people there are all so strange.

3. I'll take my horse, I'll take my rope,
   And hit the trail upon a lope.

4. Say adios to the Alamo,
   And turn my head toward Mexico.

5. I'll make my home on the wide wide range,
   For the people there are not so strange.

6. The hard hard ground shall be my bed,
   And my saddle seat shall hold my head.

Add an autoharp accompaniment to suggest the sound of the cowboy's guitar.

You will need two chords. Their names are shown above the staff. Find them on the autoharp.

Play one stroke on the **accented beat** of each **measure**.

Symphony No. 11

Movements two and four

by Henry Cowell

People often sing songs as they work, play, and worship. Composers sometimes write music about these activities.

Here are two **movements** from a **symphony** by Henry Cowell. In this symphony he describes seven activities in which people participate during their lifetime.

Listen to the second movement. It begins with a pattern played on the **timpani.** Notice how the composer creates excitement by adding instruments. Listen for a new rhythm played by **French horns.**

Can you hear other musical ideas? Do any patterns return?

Listen to the fourth movement. How many **sections** do you hear? Compare the sections. Talk about the rhythms, the melodies, and the important instruments that you notice in each section.

When you have enjoyed the two movements, discuss your ideas. What activities do you think Cowell described in his music?

The Shepherd's Song

German Folk Song
English Words Adapted

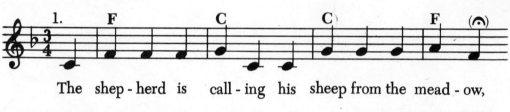

The shep - herd is   call - ing his sheep from the mead - ow,

The sound of __ his __ call can be   heard o'er __ the __ hills:

La   la   la   la   la   la   la   la, _____

la   la   la   la   la   la   la   la.

Can you learn the rhythm of "Kookaburra" and "The Shepherd's Song" by studying the notes? Follow these steps.

Will the song move in twos or in threes?
The top number of the **meter signature** will help you decide.

Next, notice how the **bar lines** group the notes into **measures**.
Can you decide which note will sound with the beat?
How many of these notes will be in a measure?

10

Can you find notes that will sound **twice as long** as the beat?

How many will be in a measure?

Can you find notes that sound **half as long** as the beat?

How many will be in a measure?

Kookaburra

Australian Round

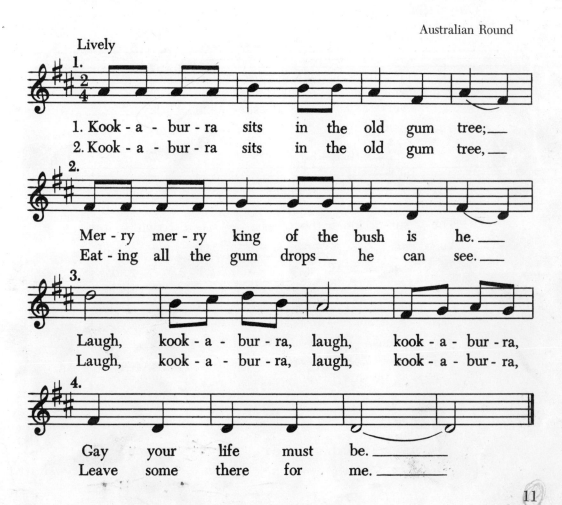

1. Kook - a - bur - ra sits in the old gum tree; ___
2. Kook - a - bur - ra sits in the old gum tree, ___

Mer - ry mer - ry king of the bush is he. ___
Eat - ing all the gum drops ___ he can see. ___

Laugh, kook - a - bur - ra, laugh, kook - a - bur - ra,
Laugh, kook - a - bur - ra, laugh, kook - a - bur - ra,

Gay your life must be. _____
Leave some there for me. _____

The Morning

Las mananitas

Mexican Folk Melody
English Words Adapted

All over the world, people celebrate special occasions with music. What song usually is sung on the occasion celebrated by this song?

How beau - ti - ful is the morn - ing; _____
Qué lin - da es - tá la ma - ña - na, _____

It's a ver - y _____ spe - cial day. _____
en que ven - go a _____ sa - lu - dar - te, _____

The sun in the east is dawn - ing, _____
Ve - ni - mos to - dos reu - ni - dos, _____

And we've come to you to say: _____
con pla - cer a fe - li - ci - tar - te, _____ Ya

Hap - py birth - day, my good {boy, girl,
vie - ne a - ma - ne - cien - do, ya

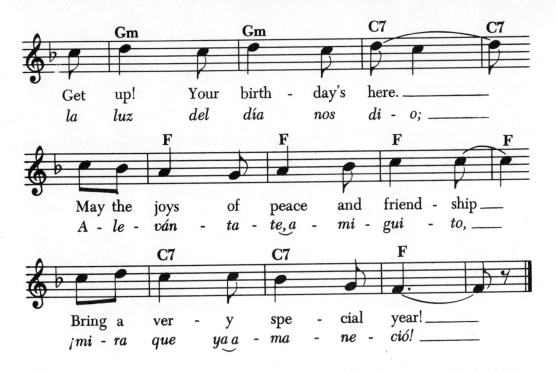

Gm	Gm	C7	C7

Get up! Your birth - day's here. _____
la luz del día nos di - o; _____

F	F	F	F

May the joys of peace and friend - ship _____
A - le - ván - ta - te, a - mi - gui - to, _____

C7	C7	F

Bring a ver - y spe - cial year! _____
¡mi - ra que ya a - ma - ne - ció! _____

Compose a Percussion Round

You can play "Kookaburra" as a percussion round.

Two people may choose instruments with contrasting sounds.

Listen for the interesting sounds that are created as you play different rhythm patterns at the same time.

You can compose your own percussion round.

Use $\frac{2}{4}$ as your meter signature.

Begin by making up different measures of rhythm.

How many different measures can you make up using these notes?

Next, put your measures in order, one after another, to make an interesting rhythm. You may use some patterns more than once.

Practice the complete composition. When you know it well, two people may play it as a round. Decide when the second person begins.

13

Quiet

Words and Music
by Malvina Reynolds

Verse

1. I don't know much a - bout much, _____
2. I've made mis - takes in the past, _____
3. I have a T. V. at home, _____

And what I don't know I don't say, And
Things that I blush o - ver yet, But
And I do tru - ly en - joy it, But

when I have noth - ing to say, I'm qui - et.
I hard - ly ev - er re - gret Hav - ing been qui - et.
I can just leave it a - lone, And it's qui - et.

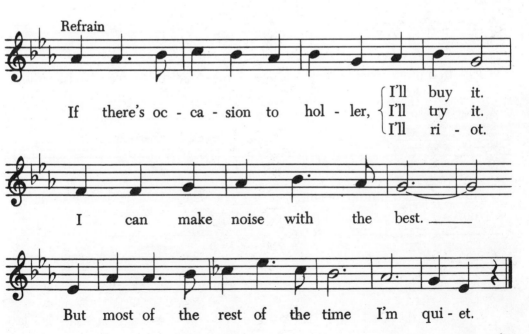

Refrain

If there's oc - ca - sion to hol - ler, { I'll buy it.
{ I'll try it.
{ I'll ri - ot.

I can make noise with the best. _____

But most of the rest of the time I'm qui - et.

15

Hiking, Laughing, Singing

Old Swedish Hiking Song

1. Let us stride a - long to - geth - er In the
hik - ing, laugh - ing, sing - ing To the

sun - ny au - tumn weath - er, Tra - la - la - la - la - la
tune with - in us ring - ing,

la - la - la - la - la - la, We are Tra - la - la - la - la - la - la -

la - la - la - la - la - la. 2. We will throw a - way mis -

giv - ing In the joy, the joy of liv - ing, As we

breeze a - long the high - ways And ex - plore for - got - ten

by - ways. If the sun fails to keep shin - ing, We will

seek the sil - ver lin - ing. Tra - la - la - la -

la - la - la - la - la - la - la - la - la - la.

Play an autoharp accompaniment as you sing.
The chords are written above the staff of verse one.
Decide what chords should be played during verse two.

You will use the same chords, but in a different order.
Your ears will help you decide.

Music of Your Own

A good way to express ideas through music is to compose music of your own. Explore the sounds of your classroom instruments. Discover different **tone qualities**.

You can experiment with one instrument or with several. You can work by yourself, with a classmate, or in groups of three or four.

Experiment with **rhythm** on different percussion instruments.

Experiment with **melody** on the bells.

Experiment with **harmony** on the autoharp.

Experiment with different musical **designs**.

1. Discover the tone qualities of different percussion instruments. Which have deep tones? Which have light tones?

   Find different ways of tapping or shaking the instrument to make different sounds.

2. Discover different rhythms to play on the instrument of your choice.

   Compose a rhythm that is even. Compose one that is uneven.

   Compose rhythms for marching, for skipping, for dancing.

   Imagine a story. Try to tell it by playing different rhythms on instruments of different tone qualities.

3. Discover the different tones of the bells.

   Play tones that are high and others that are low.

   Compose a melody using only white bells.

   Compose a melody using only black bells.

   Choose a few bells you like to hear and compose a melody using only these tones.

   Plan the **contour** of your melody before you play.

4. Compose a melody or rhythm made up of several phrases.
   Can you give your composition a design?
   Include some phrases that are the same and some that
   are different.

5. Discover the different chords of the autoharp.
   Notice the different sounds of the chords.
   Experiment with different ways of strumming the strings.

   Choose a few chords you like to hear.
   Compose a melody to sing as you play these chords.

Practice until you can remember your experiments.
Share them with the class.

Lullaby Round

Traditional Round

Can you sing this song with numbers? The melody begins on 1. How many **different** pitches will you sing? When you have learned the melody, sing the song with words. Sing it as a round.

Play the melody on the bells. Begin by putting all the bells in a row from low to high.

Call the C bell "1." Play the melody. Your ears will help you know which bells to play.

Did you play all the bells? Which ones did you omit? Which did you play? Play these again from low to high. Describe the pattern you played.

This pattern is called a **major scale**. You played the **C major scale**. When a melody is made up of tones that belong to the C major scale, we say it is in the **key of C**. C is **home tone**. C is the first step of the scale.

Once

Israeli Folk Song

This song is in the same **key** as "Lullaby Round." Can you sing it with numbers? Which **pitch** will be home tone?

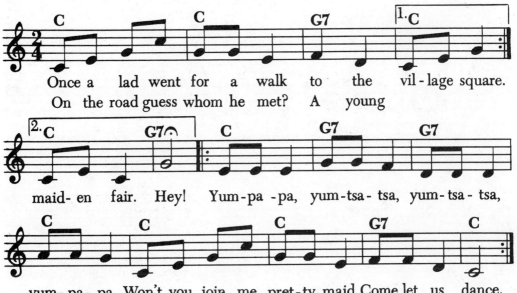

Once a lad went for a walk to the vil-lage square.
On the road guess whom he met? A young

maid- en fair. Hey! Yum-pa -pa, yum-tsa- tsa, yum-tsa- tsa,

yum- pa- pa. Won't you join me, pret-ty maid, Come let us dance.

Play this melody on the bells. When you played "Lullaby Round," your ears told you what bells to use. You can also find the correct bells in another way.

Notice that the bells are named by letters of the alphabet. The **lines** and **spaces** of the **staff** are named with the same letters.

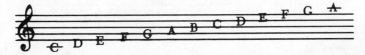

Look at the notes of the melody. Find the bells that have the same letter names as the notes. Put the bells in order from low to high. Read the notes and play the melody.

21

Holla-Hi! Holla-Ho!

German Folk Melody
Translated by Peter Kunkel

1. Who comes up the mead-ow way? } Hol - la - hi! Hol - la - ho!
2. Peo - ple say with twin-kling eyes, }

Sure - ly 'tis my sweet-heart gay; } Hol - la - hi - a - ho!
Love is blind but age makes wise; }

She goes by the _ o - pen door, } Hol - la - hi! Hol - la - ho!
Lit - tle heed I _ when they tease, }

Must not love me _ an - y - more, } Hol - la - hi - a - ho!
I may love just _ whom I please, }

Here are the pitches that are used in the melody of this song.

Give the letter name of each note. Notice that there is a low C and a high C. Both are **home tone.** Both may be called "1." What will **high D** be called?

22

America

Music Attributed to Henry Carey
Words by Samuel Francis Smith

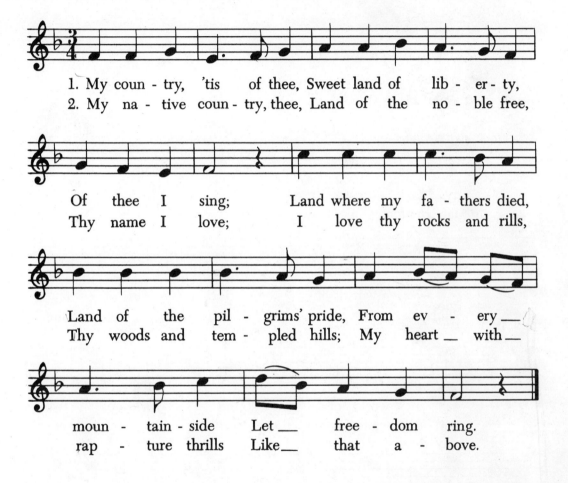

1. My coun - try, 'tis of thee, Sweet land of lib - er - ty,
2. My na - tive coun - try, thee, Land of the no - ble free,

Of thee I sing; Land where my fa - thers died,
Thy name I love; I love thy rocks and rills,

Land of the pil - grims' pride, From ev - ery __
Thy woods and tem - pled hills; My heart __ with __

moun - tain - side Let __ free - dom ring.
rap - ture thrills Like __ that a - bove.

3. Let music swell the breeze,
   And ring from all the trees
   Sweet freedom's song;
   Let mortal tongues awake;
   Let all that breathe partake;
   Let rocks their silence break;
   The sound prolong.

4. Our fathers' God, to thee,
   Author of liberty,
   To thee we sing;
   Long may our land be bright
   With freedom's holy light;
   Protect us by thy might,
   Great God, our King.

It's a Small World

Words and Music by
Richard M. Sherman
and Robert B. Sherman

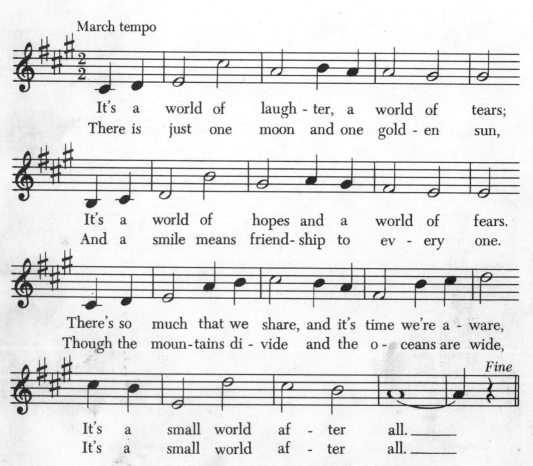

March tempo

It's a world of laugh - ter, a world of tears;
There is just one moon and one gold - en sun,

It's a world of hopes and a world of fears.
And a smile means friend-ship to ev - ery one.

There's so much that we share, and it's time we're a - ware,
Though the moun-tains di - vide and the o - ceans are wide,

Fine

It's a small world af - ter all._____
It's a small world af - ter all._____

It's a small world af - ter all,

It's a small world af - ter all,

It's a small world af - ter all,

D.C. al Fine

It's a small, small world. _____

Listen to the recording. How many **sections** do you hear? What helps you know when one section ends and a new one begins? Write the design of the sections with capital letters. Use the same letters for sections that sound the same.

How many **phrases** do you hear in each section? Can you hear phrases that sound exactly the same? that are similar? that are different?

We Sing of Golden Mornings

Music from William Walker's *Southern Harmony*
Words Adapted by Vincent Silliman
from a poem by Ralph Waldo Emerson

Brightly

1. We sing of gold-en morn-ings, We sing of spar-kling seas,
2. We sing the heart cou-ra-geous, The youth-ful, ea-ger mind;

Of prai-ries, val-leys, moun-tains, And state-ly for-est trees.
We sing of hopes un-daunt-ed, Of friend-ly ways and kind.

We sing of flash-ing sun-shine And life-be-stow-ing rain,
We sing the ros-es wait-ing Be-neath the deep-piled snow;

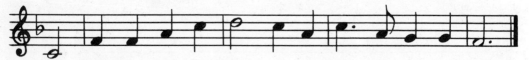

Of birds a-mong the branch-es, And spring-time come a-gain.
We sing, when night is dark-est, The day's re-turn-ing glow.

Can you decide when each phrase ends in this song by looking at the music? What helps you to know?

Write the design of the phrases with letters. The first is A.

Do you find other phrases that are similar, but not exactly the same? Call them A'.

Let's Explore Other Art

Some Uses of Poetry

by Eva Merriam

to paint without a palette
to dance without music
to speak without speaking

to feel the strangeness between hot and cold
to feel the likeness of hot and cold
to plunge into both at the same moment.

Have you ever thought that a poem could help you feel such things? Other arts also help us feel "strangeness" and "likeness." That is one purpose of art, to help us see and hear things in ways we've never thought of before.

Each art has its own materials and means of expression. Music arranges musical sounds to express ideas through rhythm, melody, and harmony. Dancers express ideas through movement. As you enjoy the painting and poetry on these pages, talk about the materials that each artist used to express his ideas.

City

by Langston Hughes

In the morning the city
Spreads its wings
Making a song
In stone that sings

In the evening the city
Goes to bed
Hanging lights
About its head

Britanny Landscape
by Paul Gauguin

The work of an artist often reflects the time and place in which he lives. He finds meaning in his own experiences. He expresses this meaning through his art. Other people enjoy his art because they have experienced the same feelings and ideas.

Do the artists who painted the picture and wrote the poetry on these pages help you understand anything about the times and places in which they lived?

Art of Your Own

On page 18 you were given suggestions for composing music of your own. Have you ever created other art of your own? Have you written a poem, painted a picture, or modeled a figure in clay or wood?

Choose an art form you like. Think about the ideas and feelings you wish to present in your art work.

What materials will you use? Will you use paints, paper, clay, wood? Will you use words or musical tones?

When you have completed your art work, share it with the class. Describe the materials and ideas with which you worked. Discuss the pleasures and problems of creating something of your own.

Dance Your Own Dance

Dancing is a good way to express your feelings and ideas. Dancing while you listen also will help you concentrate on the music.

Each person can express what he hears in the music.
Each one can dance with his own movements and develop his own ideas.

Sometimes you will want to work together to compose dances.

You can dance the rhythm of the music.
You can show the shape of the melody.
You can give your dance the design of the music.
Your dance can have the style of the music you are hearing.

Suite No. 3 in D Major

Gavotte

by Johann Sebastian Bach

More than two hundred years ago at the time of Bach, the gavotte was a favorite dance. Bach and other composers of that time wrote concert music based on this dance rhythm.

Listen to the "Gavotte," and enjoy the merry rhythm with accents in twos. Listen for the sound of the string instruments and the trumpet. Study the design of the composition. Why do we say that Bach arranged it in the design A B A?

Bach did not write this music for dancing, but you can dance to it. Experiment until you have dance patterns which you like for each melody. Discuss how you will give your dance the same design as the music. Work together and compose a dance that expresses the musical composition.

Unsquare Dance

by Dave Brubeck

Composers of today also enjoy composing dances. As you listen, can you decide why Brubeck called this the "unsquare" dance?

Bach's dance moved with accents in twos. How does the rhythm move in this dance? What instruments play important melodies? Can you find a design?

Brubeck did not compose this for dancing, but you will enjoy dancing to it. Develop steps with the rhythm. Will you dance in the same style as when you danced the "Gavotte"?

Landscape: Country Occupations and Pastimes
Detail from scroll
by Katsushika Hokusai

Music from Far Away

We like to sing the songs of our own country. We also enjoy singing songs from other countries. We like to dance to music of different lands and learn rhythms and dance patterns other people know.

Different countries have developed music with different sounds. Each country has melodies and rhythms that seem to belong especially to that country. Yet, people everywhere have songs that express similar feelings and ideas.

Artists often use materials that they find in their own lands. Their works of art reflect the life of the places where they live.

As you explore music and other arts from different lands, notice similarities and differences among these works of art and those of your own country. What similar thoughts and feelings are expressed? What materials and ideas do you find that are different?

Enjoy the arts of far away. Imagine life as it is in these distant places.

Kum Ba Yah

African Folk Song

This song comes from Africa. People everywhere enjoy singing it.

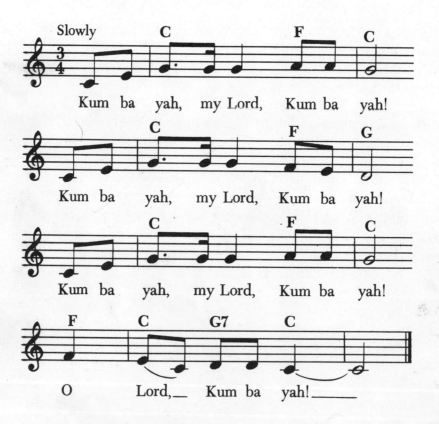

Slowly

Kum ba yah, my Lord, Kum ba yah!

Kum ba yah, my Lord, Kum ba yah!

Kum ba yah, my Lord, Kum ba yah!

O Lord,__ Kum ba yah!____

2. Someone's crying, Lord . . .
3. Someone's singing, Lord . . .
4. Someone's praying, Lord . . .

34

Indian Sitar Player

Hari Krishna

Ancient Indian Chant

This is an ancient religious chant from India. Sing it over and over. Keep a steady **tempo**. Gradually sing louder as you repeat the chant.

Ha - ri   Krish - na,   Ha - ri   Krish - na,

Krish - na,   Krish - na,   Ha - ri,   Ha - ri.

Ha - ri   Ra - ma,   Ha - ri   Ra - ma,

Ra - ma,   Ra - ma,   Ha - ri,   Ha - ri.

Add a drone accompaniment on the autoharp. Press down the G major and G minor chords at the same time. Strum often enough to keep the strings sounding steadily.

To Thee before the Close of Day

Plainsong
English Words by John M. Neale

Chants similar to this one have been sung for centuries in European churches. Notice that there is no meter signature and no bar lines. This was often true in ancient music. Sing the melody freely, accenting the words as if you were speaking them.

To thee be - fore the close of day,
Jam lu - cis or - to si - de - re,

Cre - a - tor of the world, we pray
De - um pre - ce - mur sup - pli - ces,

That, with thy wont - ed fa - vor, thou
Ut in di - ur - nis ac - ti - bus,

Wouldst be our guard and keep - er now.⎫
Nos ser - vet a no - cen - ti - bus.⎬ A - men.___
⎭

What is similar about the song on this page and those on pages 34 and 35? What differences do you notice? Compare melodies, rhythms, and harmonies.

36

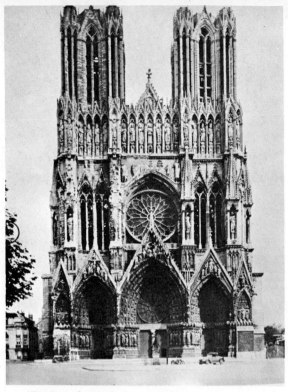

Rheims Cathedral

Carillon

from *L'Arlésienne Suite No. 1*

by Georges Bizet

A **carillon** is a set of bells hung in the steeple of a tall tower and played by means of a keyboard. Many cathedrals have carillons which are played to call the people to worship.

In Bizet's composition, the orchestra imitates the sound of a carillon. Listen to the opening section. The three-tone pattern of the bells is played by the French horns.

Can you play the pattern on the bells? You will need E, F#, G#.

Violins play this melody against the repeated bell pattern.

Listen to the complete composition. How can you tell when the middle section is about to begin? What clue tells you that the opening section is going to be repeated as the third section of the composition?

37

Little Bells of Westminster

Traditional Round

Study the melody of this song by looking at the notation. 1 is on the second line of the staff. Can you sing the melody with numbers? with words? Then sing it as a round.

The lit - tle bells of West-min- ster go ding, dong, ding, dong, dong.

What is the letter name of **home tone** for this song? Build a major scale on the bells, beginning on that tone. Begin by putting the bells in order.

Experiment until your pattern sounds like the major scale. What did you do on the seventh step?

Name all the bells you played. The seventh one should be called F sharp. This is the sign for sharp: #.

Look at the beginning of the song. Do you find a clue that tells you to play F#? This clue is the **key signature**.

The Bell Doth Toll

Traditional Round

Home tone is in the first space of the staff. Sing the song with numbers. Play it on the bells. Perform it as a round. Play one part on the bells while the other two parts are sung.

Arrange the bells in order as shown on page 38. Play the scale of this song.

What bell did you play as the fourth step? Call this **pitch** B flat. Look at the **key signature** at the beginning of the song. Can you find a sign that tells you to play B flat?

Play the scales of C, F, and G on the bells. Describe the pattern that you played each time. When did you omit bells? When did you play bells close together?

In what ways were the patterns similar? Were they different in any way?

Frogs

Shu Ha Mo

Chinese Folk Song
English Words by Betty Warner Dietz
and Thomas Choonbai Park

Briskly and lightly

1.
Each frog has a sin - gle mouth.
Yi chih ha mo yi chang tsui

2.
He has two eyes and four legs.
Liang chih yen ching szu t'iao t'ui.

3.
Ping pong ping pong { Count them with me.
{ *T'iao hsia shui ya.*

4.&5.
Dur - ing time of peace frogs do not drink.
Ha mo pu ch'ih shui t'ai p'ing nien.

6.&7.
Wa - ter lil - ies float on the pond.
Ho erh mei tzu hsi shui p'iao.

Find the bells you need to play this song. Play them from low to
high. Does this pattern sound like the scale you played on page 38?

Improvise an accompaniment on these bells while the class sings the
song as a round.

Congo Lullaby

Congo Folk Song
English Words by Carol Hart Sayre

In swaying rhythm

Yo,— yo,— yo, yo, yo, Yo,— yo,— yo, yo,

Mwa - na, dear, now do not cry, Soon will come your
Mwa - na, le - kan - ga, ku - jile, Ju - lon - de ba

ta - ta; Food he'll bring you by and by,
sho - be, I - no - be wen - de - le kwe - pi?

And per - haps a ba - ta. Yo,— yo,—
Ku - le - ta kud - ya, kud - ya

slowly

yo, yo, yo, Yo,— yo,— yo, yo, yo.

What does this song have in common with the Spanish song on page 42?

41

A la nanita nana

Spanish Folk Melody
English Words Adapted

This lullaby is known in many Spanish-speaking countries. Some of the words here are in English. The spanish words essentially mean, "Lullaby, lullaby."

A la na-ni-ta na-na, na-ni-ta e-a, na-ni-ta e-a,

An-gels your watch are keep-ing, will hush your weep-ing, bring peace-ful sleep-ing.

The night-in-gale is sing-ing, foun-tain is play-ing,

Your lit-tle cra-dle swing-ing in bran-ches sway-ing.

A la na-ni-ta na-na, na-ni-ta e - a.

A la na-ni-ta na-na, na-ni-ta e - a.

Notice that this song has two different **key signatures**. The first section of the song is based on this scale.

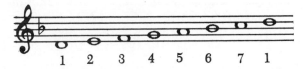

1 2 3 4 5 6 7 1

The second section is based on this scale.

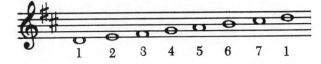

1 2 3 4 5 6 7 1

What is the same about the two scales? Describe the differences. Which one is **major**? The other is **minor**.

Sing the song. Listen carefully to the differences.

The Young Monk

Chinese Folk Song
English Words by Chin-Hsin Yao Chen
and Shih-Hsiang Chen

In earlier days Chinese parents sometimes sent their sons to monasteries so that they might grow up to be monks. The parents did this either because of religious faith or because of poverty.

Once a young— monk Went to a shrine To say his
eve - ning pray'r. Tears were in his eyes, Bit - ter his
cries, As he said his pray'r: "O Bud - dha
might - y and kind, And— all ye oth - er gods,
Help— to — go, Help me to go O - ver the

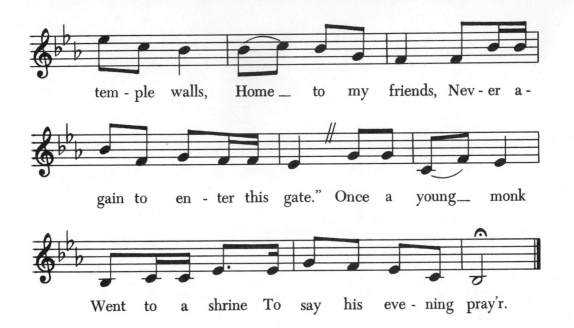

tem - ple walls, Home — to my friends, Nev - er a -

gain to en - ter this gate." Once a young — monk

Went to a shrine To say his eve - ning pray'r.

This song is based on the same scale as "The Frogs." It is called a **pentatonic** scale because it uses only five tones.

Improvise an accompaniment on bells or piano. Use any tones of the scale. Play your accompaniment in a rhythm that contrasts to the rhythm of the melody.

Variations on "Sakura"

by Kimio Eto

You may have learned a Japanese song called "Cherry Bloom" when you were in third grade. The Japanese name for that song is "Sakura." It is probably the Japanese song best known in the United States.

The **koto** player begins by playing the familiar melody. He then repeats the melody a number of times, varying it in different ways. How many **variations** do you hear? In what ways is the melody varied each time?

Au clair de la lune

French Folk Song

This song is in the same **key** as "Little Bells of Westminster."

Which step of the scale is marked with a **sharp** in the key signature? Can you locate **home tone**?

1. Au clair de la lu - ne, Mon a - mi Pier - rot,
2. Au clair de la lu - ne, Pier - rot ré - pon - dit:

Prê - te - moi ta plu - me, Pour é - crire un mot;
Je n'ai pas de plu - me. Je suis dans mon lit.

Ma chan - delle est mor - te, Je n'ai plus de feu;
Va chez la voi - si - ne, Je crois qu'elle y est,

Ou - vre - moi ta por - te, Pour l'a - mour de Dieu.
Car dans la cui - si - ne, On bat le bri - quet.

The French words mean:

1. In the moonlight, my friend Peter, give me your pen to write a note; my candle is out, I don't have a match. Open your door to me.

2. In the moonlight, Peter answered, "I don't have a pen, I am in my bed. Go to the neighbor, I think she's there in the kitchen making a fire."

46

I Have a Penny

Cancion burgalesa

Spanish Folk Song
English Words by Kurt Stone

What other song have you learned that is in the same **key** as this song? Play that scale on the bells. Sing the song with numbers. When you know the melody, listen to the recording and learn the Spanish.

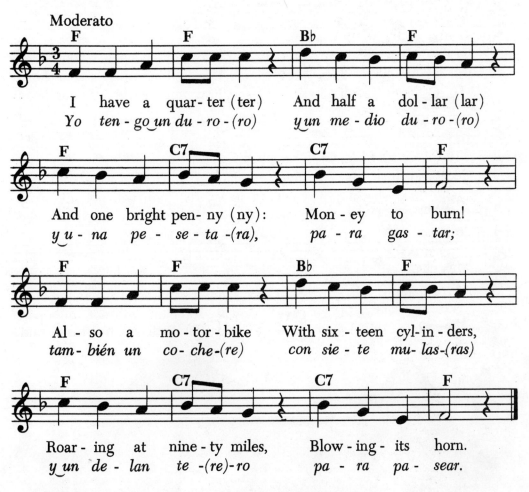

Do you think all of the words of this song are true?

Make up a new verse about something you'd like to buy with your money.

Vreneli

Swiss Folk Song

Look at the **key signature**. Notice the three flats. **The last flat is the fourth step of the scale.** Can you find **home tone**?

Play a major scale beginning on that tone. Did you include the flats shown in the key signature?

1. "O Vren - e - li, my pret- ty one, Pray tell me where's your home?"
2. "O Vren - e - li, my pret- ty one, Pray tell me where's your heart?"
3. "O Vren - e - li, my pret- ty one, Pray tell me where's your head?"

"My home it is in Swit-zer-land, It's made of wood and stone."
"O that," she said, "I gave a-way, Its pain will not de-part."
"O that, I al - so gave a-way, 'Tis with my heart," she said.

"My home it is in Swit- zer-land, It's made of wood and stone."
"O that," she said, "I gave a-way, Its pain will not de - part."
"O that, I al - so gave a-way, 'Tis with my heart," she said.

48

Refrain

Yo, ho, ho, tra - la - la - la; Yo, ho, ho, tra - la - la - la;

Yo, ho, ho, tra - la - la - la; Yo, ho, ho, tra - la - la - la;

ho, tra - la - la - la, Yo, ho, ho.

The boys may sing "Yo, ho, ho" each time these words are repeated.
Hold the last tone of each pattern while the girls sing "tra-la-la-la."
Listen to the interesting harmony created by the combined tones.

Yo, ho, ho ——————— Yo, ho, ho ———————

tra - la - la - la   tra - la - la - la

49

Where Is John?

Czechoslovakian Folk Song

Look at the key signature. **The last sharp is the seventh step of the scale.** Can you find **home tone**? Sing the song with numbers. Sing it with words.

1. Where is John? __ The old red hen has left her pen.

2. Where is John? __ The cows are in the corn a - gain.

3. Oh, John! _____

Divide into two groups and sing the song as a round.

Listen carefully to the **harmony** that your voices create when phrases one and two are sung at the same time.

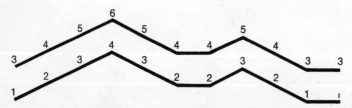

The distance between the two parts is an **interval** of a **third**.

Call John the Boatman

English Round

As you study this work song and the ones on the following pages, discuss the kinds of work found in different countries. How does music help a worker complete his task?

1. Call John the boat - man, call, call a - gain,
For loud roars the tem - pest and fast falls the rain.

2. John - ny is a good man, he sleeps so ver - y sound;
His oars are at rest and his boat is a - ground.

3. Red rolls the riv - er, so rap - id and so deep;
Well, the loud - er you call him, the fast - er he'll sleep!

Planting Rice

Philippine Folk Song

With spirit

Plant-ing rice is nev-er fun, Work from morn till set of sun, Can-not sit and can-not stand, Plant the seed-lings all by hand.

Refrain

Plant-ing rice is no fun, Work from morn till set of sun, Can-not sit, can-not stand, Plant the seed-lings all by hand.

You can sing the melody of the refrain in **thirds**. While one group sings this melody as written, a second group may sing the same melody a third lower. On what step of the scale will the second group begin? On what pitch?

In one place you will need to sing a different interval to make the harmony sound pleasing. Can you find the place? Experiment until you find a tone that harmonizes with the melody.

Rice Harvesting Song

Gao Trang

Vietnam Folk Song
English Words by Eleanor Chroman

Andante

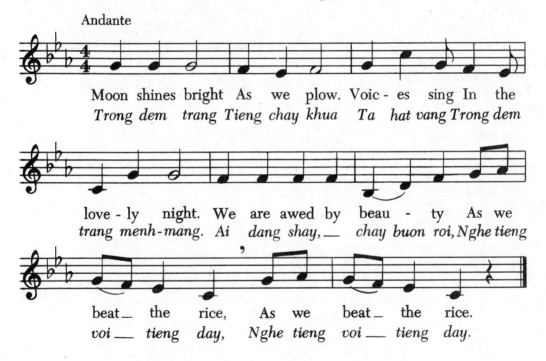

Moon shines bright As we plow. Voic - es sing In the
Trong dem trang Tieng chay khua Ta hat vang Trong dem

love - ly night. We are awed by beau - ty As we
trang menh-mang. Ai dang shay, chay buon roi, Nghe tieng

beat the rice, As we beat the rice.
voi tieng day, Nghe tieng voi tieng day.

Why would people in the Philippines and Vietnam sing songs about planting and harvesting rice? In what other countries might you find such songs?

In Vietnam everyone helps at harvest time. In the evening the people gather around bonfires to hull the rice. They sing as they work. Each person has a sack of rice which he beats against the ground with the beat of the music.

53

Laboring Song

Kwaeja no makashot (Day dawns with freight to haul)

African Folk Song

Rhythmic and spirited

Day   dawns with freight to   haul,   e - ya,   e - ya,
Kwae - ja   no   ma - ka - shot,   e - ya,   e - ya,

Day   dawns with freight to   haul,   Look for the la - bel!
kwae - ja   no   ma - ka - shot,   ji - ka ma - la - ka!

Day   dawns with freight to   haul,   e - ya,   e - ya,
Kwae - ja   no   ma - ka - shot,   e - ya,   e - ya,

Day dawns with freight to   haul,   Look for the la - bel!
kwae - ja   no   ma - ka - shot,   ji - ka ma - la - ka!

Add an accompaniment with hand clapping or drums. Play an accompaniment made up of different rhythm patterns. Use some of these or make up your own.

54

The Yoruba people of western Africa are famous for their drum music. Listen to the sound of the **dundun** or "talking-drum." By placing his arms and hands in different positions on the drum head, the drummer can produce different tones. He can reproduce the melody as well as the rhythm of sentences. This drummer is drumming Yoruba proverbs.

Experiment with drums in your classroom. Try to change the pitch by applying pressure in different places on the drum head. Play the rhythm and melody of friends' names.

Many Yoruba people came to the United States and the West Indies. Listen to three compositions composed by Michael Olatunji who now lives in this country. The first is "Jin-Go-Lo-Ba." The song tells of a duet between two drums.

"Frekoba" is a play-dance between boys and girls. The dancers must match their steps to the drummer's rhythm. Can you?

In "Oyin Momo Ado" you will hear the **sansa** or thumb piano as well as drums. The title means "Sweet as Honey."

The Happy Plowman

Swedish Folk Song
Translated by Mrs. Elbert Magnuson

1. Near a home in a wood, with a horse ver - y good,
2. In the house near the wood, where the farm - er ___ stood,

A poor young farm - er smiled as he stood;
There lived his help - mate love - ly and good.

Look - ing down at his plow, In his heart was a glow,
As she cooked and she stirred, She was glad that she heard,

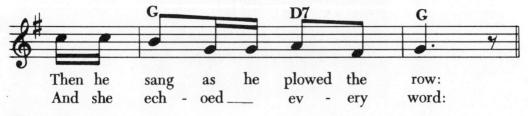

Then he sang as he plowed the row:
And she ech - oed ___ ev - ery word:

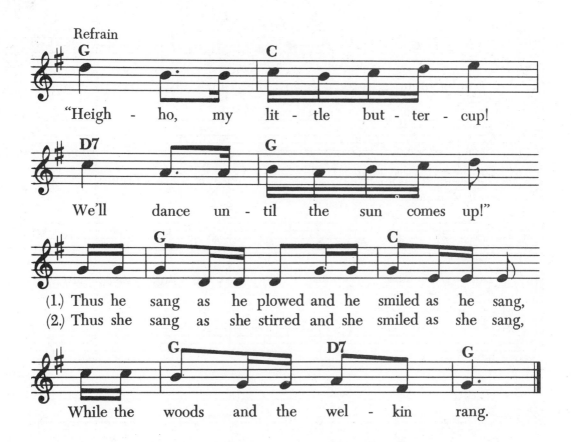

Refrain

G   C
"Heigh - ho,   my   lit - tle   but - ter - cup!

D7   G
We'll   dance   un - til   the   sun   comes   up!"

G   C
(1.) Thus he   sang   as   he plowed and he   smiled as   he   sang,
(2.) Thus she   sang   as   she stirred and she   smiled as   she   sang,

G   D7   G
While the   woods   and the   wel - kin   rang.

Songs are made up of **sections** and **phrases**. Find the sections in this song. Find the phrases.

Sometimes phrases are made up of short patterns. Here is the first pattern of phrase one: Can you find other patterns in this phrase?

57

The Caravan

Syrian Folk Song

Here is another song to sing in harmony. Listen to the recording. Tap the rhythm of the two parts. Which one usually moves with the beat? Look at the meter signature. How does this help you to know?

Tramp, tramp, heav-y go the cam - els, Tramp, tramp,

Tramp, tramp, heav - y, Tramp, tramp,

cam - els heav - y lad - en, Swing - ing, sway - ing,

heav - y, Swing - ing,

1.
on the road to Bagh - dad, Heav-y goes the car - a van.

sway - ing, Heav - y bur - den.

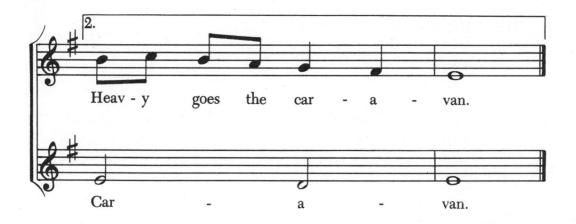

Heav - y goes the car - a - van.

Car - a - van.

How will you sing the song to express the mood suggested by the words? What in the music helps create this mood?

Two people may play an accompaniment as the class sings. Begin with these patterns. Improvise others as you continue.

High-pitched drum:

Finger cymbals:

Sponge Fishing

Greek Folk Song

The songs that people sing reflect their way of life and the lands in which they live. Why would you expect to hear fishing songs in Greece? What other work songs have you studied that help you know something about the people and the places in which they live?

Lit - tle ship, we'll go a - fish - ing Out from the shore, Out from the shore. When the eve - ning bell is ring - ing, Man - y spong-es we'll be bring - ing, And we'll sail for home with sing - ing, O - lo lo lo, o - lo lo lo.

San Serení

Spanish Folk Song

This song is really a game song, although it is about work.
Do you know an American game song that sings of work?

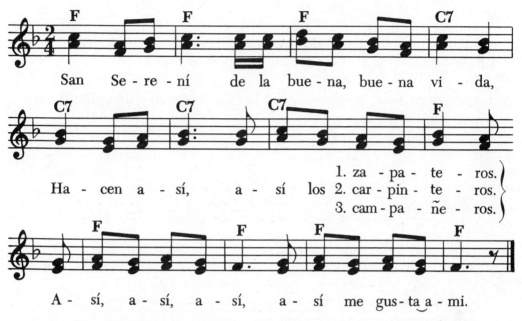

San Se - re - ní de la bue - na, bue - na vi - da,

Ha - cen a - sí, a - sí los
1. za - pa - te - ros.
2. car - pin - te - ros.
3. cam - pa - ñe - ros.

A - sí, a - sí, a - sí, a - sí me gus - ta a - mi.

4. San Serení de la buena, buena vida, Hacen así, así las planchadoras.
5. San Serení de la buena, buena vida, Hacen así, así las lavanderas . . .
6. San Serení de la buena, buena vida, Hacen así, así las costureras . . .
7. San Serení de la buena, buena vida, Hacen así, así los jardineros . . .
8. San Serení de la buena, buena vida, Hacen así, así los barquilleros.

Play this accompaniment.

De bezem

Dutch Round

The words of this round mean, "The broom, the broom, what do you do with it? We sweep the floor!" Do you think this is a work song? Why do you enjoy singing it?

Listen to the recording. How does the rhythm move? Look at the meter signature. Is it the one you expected to see?

Locate **home tone.** Remember, **the last flat in the key signature is the fourth step of the scale.**

Look at the melody. Why will it be easy to learn?

1. De be - zem, de be - zem,

2. Wat doe je er mee? Wat doe je er mee?

3. Wij ve - gen er mee, Wij ve - gen er mee,

4. De vloer aan, de vloer aan!

The Cuckoo

Austrian Folk Song

1. O I went to Pe - ter's flow - ing spring Where the
2. Af - ter Eas - ter come — sun - ny days That will
3. When I've mar - ried my — maid - en fair, What then

wa - ter's so good, And I heard there the
melt all the snow; Then I'll mar - ry my
can I de - sire? O a home for her

cuck - oo As she called from the wood.
maid - en fair, We'll be hap - py, I know.
tend - ing And some wood for the fire.

Refrain

Ho - li - ah, Ho - le - rah- hi - hi - ah, Ho - le- rah cuck-oo!

Ho - le- rah-hi - hi - ah, Ho-le-rah cuck-oo! Ho - le-rah-hi - hi - ah,

Ho - le-rah cuck-oo! Ho - le- rah- hi-hi - ah - ho!

Háry János Suite

by Zoltán Kodály

This music is based on tales about a Hungarian folk character, Háry János, who would be called "Johnny" in English. He is a lovable person who likes to tell tall tales. The tales are quite unbelievable, but Johnny always makes himself the hero and everyone who listens is amused.

Prelude

There is a superstition in Hungary that, if a storyteller sneezes while speaking, every word of the story will be true! The prelude is unusual music composed of an orchestral "sneeze" and one little ten-note melody. Listen to the composition, and discuss how the "sneeze" is produced by the orchestra. Discuss all the ways in which the melody is played.

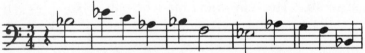

Can you hear the **theme** played in turn by the double basses, cellos, violas, and violins? Can you hear only the first five notes of the theme played by the clarinet, oboe, flute, and strings? What instrument plays the entire theme again?

What gives the music a mood of mystery? How does the music seem to say "And now the tale begins"?

64

Viennese Musical Clock

When Johnny went to Vienna, he saw the famous clock on the tower. As you might expect, Johnny's description of it was different from that of anyone else. For him the mechanical figures not only marched around, but they also did tricks!

In the musical description of Johnny's tale, the composer used percussion instruments to imitate the clock: bells, chimes, triangle, snare drums, gong, celesta, and piano. Which group of orchestral instruments plays the main theme? Which instruments play passages that add humor and excitement?

When you know the music, compose a group dance. What formation might you use to represent the mechanical figures of the clock? How will you show the many repetitions of the main theme? How will you make your dance humorous?

The Battle and Defeat of Napoleon

In this musical description, you will be able to hear Johnny's next big adventure. He and his awkward peasant army come upon the French army led by Napoleon. Johnny and his men draw their swords, and the French begin to fall in battle. Finally Napoleon must face the brave and tall Johnny. According to Johnny, Napoleon was shaking with fright and begging for mercy.

Listen to the music and follow the story in the sound of the instruments: the snare and bass drums in the introduction, three trombones to represent Johnny and his men, trombones and tuba sounding the theme of Napoleon's forces, the trumpet call to battle, the mournful music of the alto saxophone.

Mister Urian

Music by Ludwig van Beethoven
Words Translated by Ronald Duncan

Sometimes composers like to write music which is "just for fun."
They try to express humor through words and music. How does the
composer, Beethoven, express humor in this song? What other music
have you enjoyed that is humorous?

1. To trav - el is to miss the way
2. I went to see the North - ern Lights

And reach the odd - est plac - es.
Up - on an Arc - tic cruise, sir;

One day I left my home _ be - hind,
But ev - ery - thing was dark _ as _ night

But took a - long my brac - es.
Be - cause there'd been a fuse, _ sir.

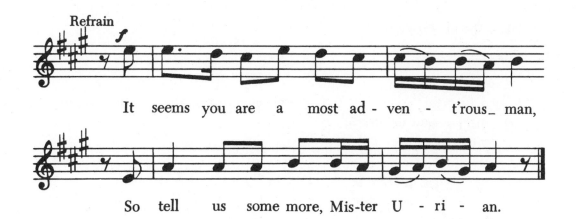

Refrain

It seems you are a most ad - ven - t'rous _ man,

So tell us some more, Mis-ter U - ri - an.

3. Then off I went to Timbucktoo
   With pockets full of carrots.
   I couldn't find a donkey there;
   I sold them to some parrots.
   Refrain

4. Of course I went to Paris, too,
   To eat some frogs and garlic.
   But it was dark when I arrived—
   I dined on dogs in aspic.
   Refrain

5. In Spain I tried to find Berlin
   But found that they had moved it;
   I bought a map of Italy
   Which only went to prove it.
   Refrain

6. From there I went to Pimlico
   To try my hand at crime, sir.
   I landed up at Wormwood Scrubs
   And there I learned to rhyme, sir.
   Refrain

Sim Sala Bim

Danish Folk Song

Notice that this song uses two meter signatures! The rhythm moves both in twos and in threes.

To feel the changing meter, tap the beat this way.

knees   hands   hands   shoulders hands

Chant the words of the song as you tap.

1. High in a tree a crow - ow - ow,
2. Then came a wick - ed hunt - er a -
3. He shot that poor old crow - ow - ow,

Sim   sa - la - bim bam boom, sa - la - doo, sa - la - dim!

High   in   a   tree a   crow- ow - ow   sat.
Then came a wick- ed   hunt - er a   -   long.
He   shot that poor old   crow- ow - ow   dead.

4. Then came a pretty maiden a-. . . long.
5. She took that poor old crow-ow-ow . . . home.
6. Now comes the happy ending: . . . soup!

Play the autoharp accompaniment. Be sure to play on the **accented beat** of each measure. Boys may sing this chant.

Sing three times:

Sim   sa - la bim,   Sim bim,

Bluebird

Parangsai

Ancient Korean Folk Song

Here is a faraway song which is also a song of long ago. It is one of the oldest folk songs still sung in Korea today. It probably first was sung nearly two thousand years ago.

Gently, in a moderate tempo

1. Blue - bird, blue - bird, love - ly blue - bird,
Sae - ya - sae - ya, pa - rang - sae - ya.
2. If the flow'r falls, no bean will grow.

Do not dis - turb flow'r - ing bean plant.
Nok - du but - te an - chi ma - ra.
Jel - ly ma - ker_____ 'll go home in tears.

People often express their feelings about nature through music and other arts. Enjoy the music on pages 70 through 73 that concern subjects of nature. Look through your book. Can you find examples of nature in painting or poetry?

69

The Butterfly

Music by Franz Schubert
Words Translated by Iris Rogers

Here is a song about a butterfly by a famous composer. On page 72 you will learn a folk song from Argentina about the same topic.

1. I dance — in the sun - shine So
2. What joy — to be danc - ing, As

free - ly and light - ly, And through — wav-ing branch - es
care - free I wan - der From morn - ing to eve - ning

Col - ors shim - mer bright - ly. Bright- er, ev - er bright - er,
O - ver hills and yon - der. When the sun is sink - ing,

See my wings are glow - ing; Sweet - er, ev - er —
Breez - es mur - mur light - ly; Woods and fields — are —

sweet - er Scent - ed buds are blow - ing.
green - er, Flow - ers glow more bright - ly.

I   plun - der their trea - sure, And feast __ at   my plea-sure,

I   plun - der their trea - sure, And feast__ at   my plea - sure.

As nature's musicians, birds have fascinated many composers. Sometimes composers suggest the songs of birds in their music. Enjoy these two compositions which include bird songs.

The Cuckoo and the Nightingale

from *Organ Concerto No. 13 in F Major*

by George Frideric Handel

Listen for the songs of the two birds named in the title. Discuss how the sounds are made.

The Pines of the Janiculum

from *The Pines of Rome*

by Ottorino Respighi

This composer also used the nightingale's song in his composition. Listen to the recording. Is the song produced in the same way as in "The Cuckoo and the Nightingale"?

Here is a melody sung by a different bird. Use it or others you know, and create your own "bird music."

71

La mariposita

Argentine Folk Song

Allegretto

1. Ma - ri - po - si - ta, de la flor,

no co - mas to - do su o - lor;

si no la tra - tas con a - mor,

se mo - ri - rá pron - to de do - lor.

When you know the melody, some of you may add harmony by singing this chant.

Ma - ri - po - si - ta, flor!   Ma - ri - po - si - ta, flor!

Ma - ri - po - si - ta, flor!   de do - lor.

The Firefly

Japanese Folk Song
English Words by Donald Paul Beyer

Come here! Come, fire - fly,

The wa - ter there is too bit - ter to drink.

The wa - ter here is much bet - ter, I think.

Come here! Come, fire - fly.

Through the moun - tain glen —

watch for the lamps to guide you

safe - ly home a - gain.

Music of Your Own

You have learned songs from many faraway lands. You have learned that people of all lands sing about similar things such as work, play, worship, love of country and home. Can you recognize the music from different places by its sound? What helps you to know that a song is from China, or Mexico? Why wouldn't you think it came from Switzerland? When we say a composition is "typical" of a certain country, we are talking about musical **style**.

Listen again to music of different countries. Try to identify the country by the sound of the music. Talk about the differences in melody, rhythm, and harmony. Notice the different instruments that are used.

Imagine you live in the Far East, Africa, or Latin America. Can you compose a song which sounds like music from one of these faraway places?

Choose a topic for your song that you think people in that country might choose. Write words for your song.

Make up a melody for your words. What scale might you use? Will it be major, minor, or pentatonic?

What rhythms will you use? Will you add harmony?

Make up an accompaniment. What instruments might imitate the sound of instruments used in the country you have chosen?

Dances from Far Away

People everywhere enjoy dancing. The dances on this page are from Denmark and Sweden, two countries that are very near each other.

The Crested Hen

Danish Folk Dance

This dance gets its name from the pointed caps the boys wear as they dance. The caps look like the crest of a hen.

Dance in groups of three. In the A section each group dances in a circle with step-hop-step-hop. In the B section dancers take turns skipping under arches made by the other two dancers. Before you begin to dance, listen to the music. Decide how many times each pattern is danced.

Gustaf's Skoal

Swedish Folk Dance
Words by Neva L. Boyd

This dance is named for the king of Sweden. For over four hundred years, the kings in that country have been named Gustaf. "Skoal" means, "We pledge a toast."

Listen to the music. How many sections are there? Will you dance in the same style in each section?

Weggis Dance

Swiss Folk Dance

1. From Lu - cerne to ___ Weg - gis fair,
2. When we row a - cross the bay,
3. Weg - gis leads to a moun - tain high,

Hol - di - ri - di - a, hol - di - ri - a,

Shoes and stock - ings we need not wear,
There we see pret - ty maid - ens gay,
Gai - ly sing as ___ we go by,

Hol - di - ri - di - a, hol - di - a.

Refrain

Hol - di - ri - di - a, Hol - di - ri - di - a, hol - di - ri - a;

Hol - di - ri - di - a, Hol - di - ri - di - a, hol - di - a.

Siva Siva Maia

Samoan Folk Song

Can you discover **home tone** by studying the key signature? Be sure to notice the B flat.

Look at the sign in measure three. This tells you to sing B natural instead of B flat. Play the two pitches on the bells. Which is higher?

The words of the first verse mean, "Come shake, time for fun and singing, shake up and down." The second verse says, "Come laugh." The third verse says, "Come dance." When you know the song, plan your own dance.

Art from Far Away

You have been learning music from far away. You have discovered that music of different lands is similar in some ways and different in others. You have discovered that learning music of a country helps you imagine life in that country.

The other arts also help us understand people from far away. By noticing the materials artists use in different parts of the world, we can understand something about the lands in which they live.

As we enjoy their paintings, sculpture, and poetry, we can learn about the activities in which they participate, and the ideas they feel are important.

Study the examples on these pages. What does each work of art help you know about the person who created it and the land in which he lived?

Dahomean Royal Procession

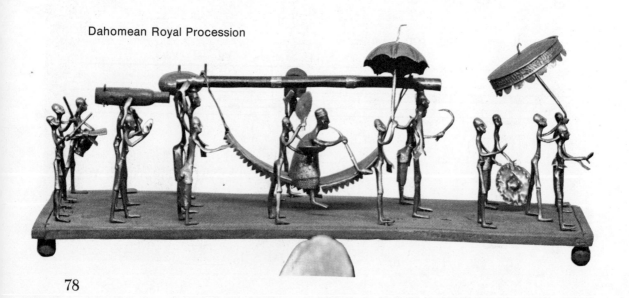

Singing Man
by Ernst Barlach

Translucent Woven Wall
by Olga De Amaral, Bogota, Colombia

Ceremonial Vessel
in the Form of an Elephant
Chinese, Shang, No. 36.6

The three buildings on this page are all places of worship. Architecture is another important art form. Study the three examples. Do they tell you anything about the importance of worship in the lives of people? Are there other things you can imagine about life in these lands as you look at the architecture?

Temple of the Sun
Palenque, Mexico

Coventry Cathedral

Japanese Pagoda

The poems on this page come from three different parts of the world. Read the poems aloud. Discuss the ideas each is trying to express.

Does each poem help you to know the poet, or to learn about life in the country where he lived?

Coming along the mountain path—
Down there a castle-town,
Many kites a-flying.

Taigi (18th century)

Good Advice

Don't shirk
Your work
For the sake of a dream;
A fish
In the dish
Is worth ten in the stream

Germany
English adapted by
Louis Untermeyer

The Moon Always Follows the Sun

Calm down, little brother,
Time heals all wounds.
No matter how much one is weeping,
The moon always follows the sun.
Eat your bananas and fresh leaves,
And don't cry any more,
Because forever and ever
The moon will follow the sun.

Congo

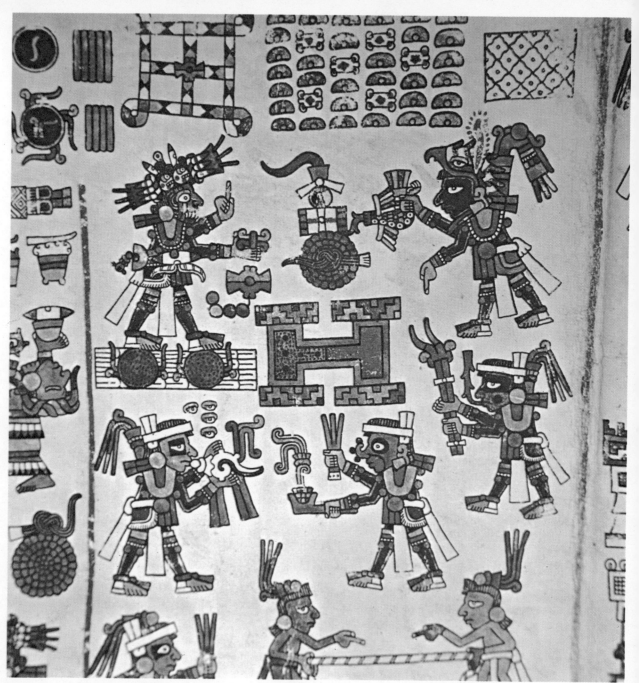

Detail from Codex
Vindobonensis Mexicanus I

Music of Long Ago

The music of each period of history seems to have its own special style. Composers who lived at different times based their music on ideas that were important in their day. They developed their own ways of organizing musical sounds. They wrote music for instruments that were known at that time.

Other arts of each period in history also reflect the style of the time. Painters, poets, and sculptors chose themes for their art that were familiar to the people of that time. They used materials that were available in their day. They organized these materials in special ways that reflected the life around them.

As you explore the music and other arts of long ago, compare the works of art with those of your own time. Are similar thoughts and feelings expressed? Do the artists use different kinds of materials? Do they organize their arts in different ways?

As you explore music and art of long ago, imagine the life of people who lived at that time.

Aztec Hymn to the Sun

Aztec Indian Prayer

Solemnly

Ah, _____ Ah, _____

Ah, ___ ah, ___ Ah, ___ ah. ___ Fine

1. Com - eth now the ris - ing sun!
2. Glo - rious shines the gold - en one!

D.C. al Fine

Praise ye him, praise ye him, might - y sun!
Praise ye him, praise ye him, might - y sun!

Hau-Wari

American Indian Lullaby

The songs on these pages and on pages 86 and 87 were sung by the people who lived in North America and South America long before these lands were settled by Europeans.

As you learn these songs, compare them to the ones you learned when studying music from far away. Do they express similar feelings and ideas? Compare melodies, rhythms, and harmonies.

Ha - u - o   Ha - u - o____   Ha - u - o____   Ha - u - wa - ri,

Ha - u - wa - ri,   Ha - u - wa - ri,   Ha - u - wa - ri

From "The Indians' Book" by Natalie Curtis, Copyright 1907, 1923 and renewed in 1950 by Dover Publications, Inc., New York. Reprinted by permission.

Athapascan Indian
Bear-Raven Song

Transcribed and Arranged
by Louis W. Ballard

Athapascan Mask
Alaska

The Athapascan Indians are from Alaska. This song is part of a dance-drama that tells the story of a foolish hunter whose first victim was a female grizzly bear! Dramatize the song when you have learned it.

E - ay - hoo, e - ay - hoo, e - ay - hoo, e - ay.

E - ay - hoo, e - ay - hoo, e - ay - ha' hah.

E - ay - ha' hah. E - ay - ha' hah. ha!

A little faster

E - ay - hoo, e - ay - hoo, e - ay - hoo e - ay.

E - ay - hoo, e - ay - hoo, e - ay - ha' hah.

E - ay - ha' hah. E - ay - ha' hah. hah!

Quapaw Indian Face-Dance Song

Transcribed and Arranged
by Louis W. Ballard

The words of this song have no meaning. It is a happy dance to be performed on social occasions. Men and women face each other as they chant and dance. When you know the music, make up your own dance to it.

Ha - na t'si wah, Ha - na ___ t'si wah, ___

Ha - na ___ t'si wah, Ha - na t'si wah.

Yo - ho wa - ni na - ah yo - ha hey,

Yo - ho wa - ni na yo - ha hey,

Yo - ho wa - ni na - ah yo - ha hey.

Why Shouldn't My Goose?

Traditional Round

The song on this page and those on pages 89 through 97 were first sung by people who lived in England long ago. This was the time when kings and nobles lived in castles, and knights fought battles to help the peasants and to win fair ladies.

As you learn the songs, try to imagine life at that time. Did the people enjoy music for the same reasons you do?

Why should-n't my goose Grow as fat as thy goose,

When I paid for my goose Twice as much as thine?

Can you learn this song by yourselves? Begin by studying the rhythm. How will it move? What note sounds with the beat? Chant the words and tap the beat.

Can you find **home tone**? If not, look at page 39. Then look at the notes. Why will this melody be easy to learn?

When you know the melody and rhythm, sing this song as a round.

Cherries So Ripe

Traditional Round

As peddlers pushed their carts through the streets of London, they would sing out to let people know that they had fresh fruits or vegetables to sell. Can you think of a way we use music today to help sell products?

Cher - ries so ripe and so round, The best in the mar-ket __

found, On - ly a pen - ny a pound. Who will buy?

Find the patterns which include dotted notes.
How long should each be held?
Study these patterns to help you decide.

Music for Ancient Instruments

Most of the instruments you hear today in bands and orchestras were developed from older instruments which were played more than five hundred years ago. Listen to music played on these ancient instruments. Can you think of modern instruments that have similar sounds?

Ductia

Anonymous

This music is played by an **oboe,** a **crumhorn,** and a **tambourine.** The tambourine is a two-headed drum. The crumhorn and the oboe have double reeds in the mouthpiece which give a distinctive sound. The oboe plays the higher melody; the crumhorn plays the lower part.

As you listen to the music, count the sections. Do any repeat the same melody? Do you hear repeated patterns within sections?

Group of Ancient
Musicians

The ductia was a kind of dance. At first these dances were danced in a circle without partners; everyone, old and young, joined in.

When you know the music, dance as the people did long ago.

Galliarde "La rocque"

Anonymous

This music is played on recorders and viols. Recorders are flute-like instruments made of wood. The viol was a string instrument. Viols and recorders were made in different sizes. The larger the instrument, the lower its range of pitches.

The galliarde was also a popular dance of long ago. It is a couple dance. Sometimes during the dance, one partner danced a solo. The man's dance was vigorous with strong leaps. The lady danced more sedately.

Plan a dance to fit the rhythm and phrasing of the music. Dance with a partner. At times during the dance, each partner may improvise his own solo.

91

The Wraggle-Taggle Gypsies

Old English Ballad

This **ballad** may have been sung first by a troubadour nearly a thousand years ago! When you have learned this ballad and the one on page 94, make your own definition of a ballad. How is it different from other songs?

1. There — were three gyp - sies a - come to my door,
2. Then — she pulled off her — silk fin - ished - gown,
3. It was late last night when my lord came — home,

And down - stairs ran this - a la - dy, O!
And put on hose of — leath - er, O!
In - quir - ing for his — la - dy, O!

The one sang high, and an - oth - er sang low,
The rag - ged rags a - bout — our door,
The ser - vants said on — ev - ery hand,

And the oth - er sang, "Bon - ny, bon - ny Bis - cay, O!"
And she's gone — with the wrag - gle - tag - gle gyp - sies, O!
"She's gone — with the wrag - gle - tag - gle gyp - sies, O!"

4. Come saddle to me my milk-white steed,
   And go and seek my pony, O!
   That I may ride and seek my bride,
   Who is gone with the wraggle-taggle gypsies, O!

5. Then he rode high, and he rode low,
   He rode through wood and copses too.
   Until he came to an open field,
   And there he espied his-a lady, O!

6. "What makes you leave your house and your land?
   What makes you leave your money, O!
   What makes you leave your new-wedded lord,
   To go with the wraggle-taggle gypsies, O!"

7. "What care I for my house and my land?
   And what care I for my money, O!
   What care I for my new-wedded lord?
   I'm off with the wraggle-taggle gypsies, O!"

8. "Last night you slept in a goose-feather bed
   With the sheet turned down so bravely, O!
   But tonight you sleep in a cold, open field
   Along with the wraggle-taggle gypsies, O!"

9. "Oh, what care I for a goose-feather bed
   With the sheet turned down so bravely, O!
   For tonight I shall sleep in a cold, open field,
   Along with the wraggle-taggle gypsies, O!"

Sir Eglamore

Old English Ballad

In the recording of this song you can hear four ancient instruments: a **rauschpfeife,** a **cornett,** a **regal organ,** and a **viola da gamba.**

Study the notation. Look at the words of the song. How many **phrases** do you find? Write the design with letters. Why does knowing the design help you learn the song?

1. Sir Eg - la - more,__ that val - iant knight, Fa   la
2. There starts a huge drag - on out of his den, Fa   la

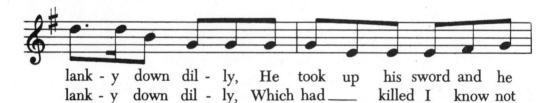

lank - y down dil - ly,   He took up   his sword and he
lank - y down dil - ly,   Which had__   killed I   know not

went for to fight; Fa la lank-y down dil-ly,
how man-y men; Fa la lank-y down dil-ly,

And as he rode o'er hill and dale, All
But when he saw Sir Eg-la-more, If

arm-èd with a coat of mail,
you'd but heard how the drag-on did roar!

Refrain

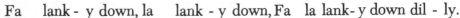

Fa lank-y down, la lank-y down, Fa la lank-y down dil-ly.

3. This dragon had a plaguey hard hide,
   Fa la lanky down dilly,
   Which could the strongest steel abide;
   Fa la lanky down dilly,
   But as the dragon yawning did fall,
   He thrust his sword down hilt and all,
   Refrain

4. The dragon laid him down and roared,
   Fa la lanky down dilly,
   The knight was sorry for his sword;
   Fa la lanky down dilly,
   The sword it was a right good blade,
   As ever Turk or Spaniard made,
   Refrain

Troubadour Song

Music by Colin Muset
Words by William S. Haynie

Troubadours were wandering musicians who traveled about the country giving news and entertaining in song. They were always welcome in the castles. For their entertainment they received food and lodging.

When cold is the wind, I look for a friend
And there I would stay, no mon - ey to pay,

To give a sing - er a room for the night.
And then be gone with the dawn's ear - ly light.

I'll play on my lute a ron - deau sweet,

If my host will give me food to eat.

Roast pheas - ant and quail, fat duck - ling and hens,

Rich cheese and mut - ton would make us good friends.

The Riddle Song

American Folk Song

1. I gave my love a cher - ry that has no stone;
2. How can there be a cher - ry that has no stone?
3. A cher - ry when it's bloom - ing, it has no stone;

I gave my love a chick - en that has no __ bone;
How can there be a chick - en that has no __ bone?
A chick - en when it's pip - ping, it has no __ bone;

I gave my love a ring __ that has no __ end;
How can there be a ring __ that has no __ end?
A ring __ when it's roll - ing it has no __ end;

I gave my love a ba - by, there's no cry - en.
How can there be a ba - by, there's no cry - en?
A ba - by when it's sleep - ing, there's no cry - en.

Musical Scales

You have learned ancient songs based on the **pentatonic scale**. Other music of long ago and today is based on **major** or **minor** scales. Play these scales. Name each one. Then look at the songs on pages 97, 100, and 101. Each song is based on a scale you played. Match the song with the correct scale.

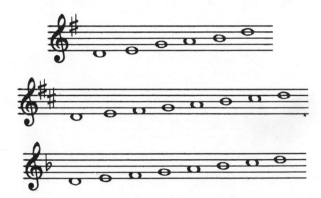

When we learn a new melody, we must know the scale on which it is based. Play a major scale beginning on the tone G. Which step in the scale did you "sharp"? Give the number of the step and the letter name of the note. Find the key signature that shows that sharp. Play the major scales beginning on A and E and answer the same questions.

What step was always sharped in **every** scale? Where is the sharp for that step placed in **every** key signature? Make up a rule that will tell you how to find **home tone** of a major scale when the key signature is in sharps.

Apply your rule to the song on page 11. Can you name the home tone? To test your answer, look at the notes of the song. Put them in order from low to high on the staff. Play them on the bells. Does the pattern sound like the scale you named? Sing the song with numbers. Does it often return to steps 1, 3, or 5? If not, you may have named the wrong scale.

Play scales beginning on A♭, D♭, E♭. Find the key signature that matches each.

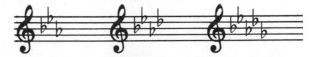

What step was always flatted in **every** scale? Where is the flat for that step placed in **every** key signature? Make up a rule for finding **home tone** when the key signature includes flats. Test your rule with the song on page 106.

My Lord, What a Morning

Spiritual

What feeling is expressed in this song?
Did you learn songs of far away that convey similar feelings?

My Lord, what a morn-ing, My Lord, what a morn-ing,

Fine

My Lord, what a morn-ing, When the stars be-gin to fall.

1. You'll hear the trum-pet sound
2. You'll hear the sin - ners mourn } To wake the na - tions un-der-ground,
3. You'll hear the Chris-tians shout

D.C. al Fine

Look-ing to my God's right hand, When the stars be-gin to fall.

The Shanty Boys in the Pine

Lumberjack Song

As you learn this work song of long ago and the ones on pages 102, 103, and 106, discuss the reasons people sing while they work. What do these work songs help you know about the people who sang them?

1. Come all   ye jol - ly shan - ty boys, come lis - ten to   my   song; __
2. The chop-pers and the saw - yers, they lay the tim-ber low, __
3. The bro - ken ice is float - ing, and sun - ny is the sky; __

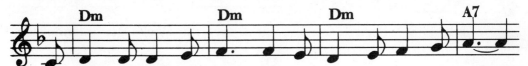

It's all   a - bout the shan - ties and how they get a - long. __
The skid - ders and the swamp - ers, they hol - ler to   and fro, __
Three hun - dred big and strong men are want - ed on   the drive. __

They are   a   jol - ly crew of boys, so mer - ry and so fine, __
And then there come the load - ers, be - fore the break of day; __
With cant hooks and with jam   - pikes these no - ble men do go, __

Who while a - way the win - ters a - cut-ting down the pine. __
Come load __ up the teams, boys, and to   the woods a - way. __
And risk their lives each spring - time on some big stream you know. __

Rock Island Line

Work Song

With a steady beat

I say the Rock Is - land Line ___ is a

might - y good road, ___ I say the Rock Is - land Line ___

___ is the road to ride; Oh, the Rock Is - land Line ___

___ is a might - y good road, ___ If you want to

ride it, got to ride it like you're fly - in'; Buy your

tick - et at the sta - tion on the Rock Is - land Line.

The Railroad Corral

Cowboy Song

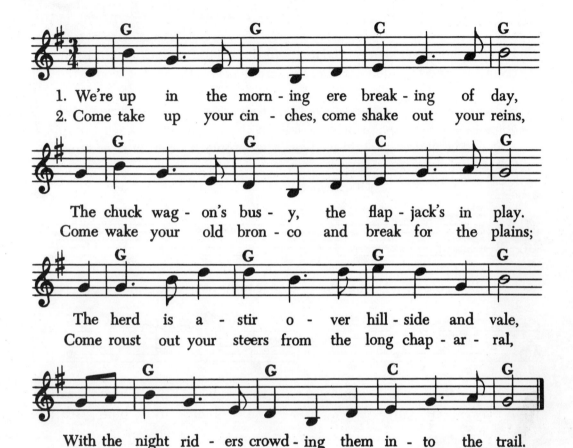

1. We're up in the morn - ing ere break - ing of day,
2. Come take up your cin - ches, come shake out your reins,

The chuck wag - on's bus - y, the flap - jack's in play.
Come wake your old bron - co and break for the plains;

The herd is a - stir o - ver hill - side and vale,
Come roust out your steers from the long chap - ar - ral,

With the night rid - ers crowd - ing them in - to the trail.
For the out - fit is off to the rail - road cor - ral.

3. The afternoon shadows are startin' to lean
   When the chuck wagon sticks in the marshy ravine;
   The herds scatter farther than vision can look,
   You can bet all true punchers will help out the cook.

4. The longest of days must reach evening at last,
   The mountains all climbed and the creeks all are past;
   The herd is a-drooping and fast falls the night,
   Let them droop if they will, for the railroad's in sight!

Blow the Wind Southerly

Northumberland Folk Song

Look at the meter signature. How will the rhythm move? Listen to the recording and tap the beat. Does it sound as you thought it would?

Notice that many measures have two groups of notes, with three eighth notes in each group. An accent falls at the beginning of each group. This makes the song sound in twos. Many songs written in sixes sound this way.

Blow the wind south- er - ly, south- er - ly, south- er - ly,

1. Blow the wind south o'er the bon - ny blue sea;
2. Blow, bon - ny breeze o'er the bon - ny blue sea;

Blow the wind south - er - ly, south- er - ly, south- er - ly,

Blow, bon - ny breeze, __ my lov - er to me. They
Blow, bon - ny breeze, __ and bring him to me.

told me last night there were ships in the off - ing, And
Is it not sweet ___ to hear the breeze sing - ing, As

I hur - ried down to the deep roll - ing sea. But my
light - ly it comes o'er the deep roll - ing sea? But ___

eye could not see it where-ev - er might be it, The
sweet - er and dear - er by far when 'tis bring - ing The

bark that is bear - ing my lov - er to me.
bark of my true love in safe - ty to me.

The Young Voyageur

Canadian Folk Melody
Words by John Andrews

Before you learn to sing this song, study its design. The design of a song
is like a chain. It is made up of many small parts linked together to
form a complete composition. Each part is essential to the whole.

Begin by finding the smallest link, which is a **motive.** A motive is a short
pattern of rhythm or melody. Here is the first rhythmic motive of this
song.

Is this rhythmic motive repeated? Is its melody repeated? Find other
motives.

Motives are linked together to form a **phrase.** How many phrases do you
find?

Phrases are grouped together to form a **section.** How many sections can
you find in this song?

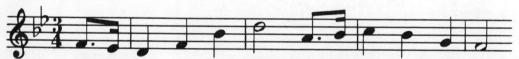

1. Oh, the voy - a - geur bold from the north-land so cold,
2. Oh, this voy - a - geur dreams of the for - est and streams;

See the wild game he takes from the riv - ers and lakes.
Rough the por - tage and long, but he still sings his song.

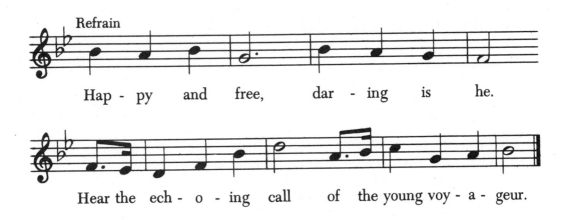

Refrain

Hap - py and free, dar - ing is he.

Hear the ech - o - ing call of the young voy - a - geur.

Some members of the class may sing this descant with the refrain.

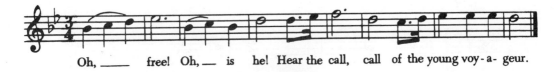

Oh, ___ free! Oh, ___ is he! Hear the call, call of the young voy - a- geur.

String Quartet No. 10 in C Major

First Movement

by Wolfgang Amadeus Mozart

Listen to this music for string quartet written by Mozart, a composer born in 1756. A string quartet is made up of two violins, a viola, and a cello. In this composition the first violin plays the main melody. Notice when other instruments have important parts.

Now become better acquainted with the melody which is the theme. It is in two parts: A, repeated and B, repeated. Here is the beginning of each part of the theme.

Listen again and discover the different ways Mozart uses this melody. First it is played. Then it is played differently four times. The new sections are called **variations.**

Now listen to each variation. How is the theme changed? New notes may be added to the melody. Sometimes the accompaniment is different. The rhythm may be changed. Describe all that you hear in each variation.

Listen again to the complete composition. What happens after the fourth variation? How many sections are in the complete composition?

Music of Your Own

The design which Mozart used in his string quartet is a very old one. Here is an ancient folk melody. Compose a set of **variations** of your own. Use this melody as your theme.

Create a variation by adding harmonizing tones to the melody.

Make another variation by changing the rhythm. Play the melody in a different meter. You might use changing meters.

Play the melody in a minor key.

Give your melody a new sound by playing some of the tones in a different **octave**.

Practice each variation until it pleases you and you know it by heart. Then start with the theme and play the variations as a complete composition.

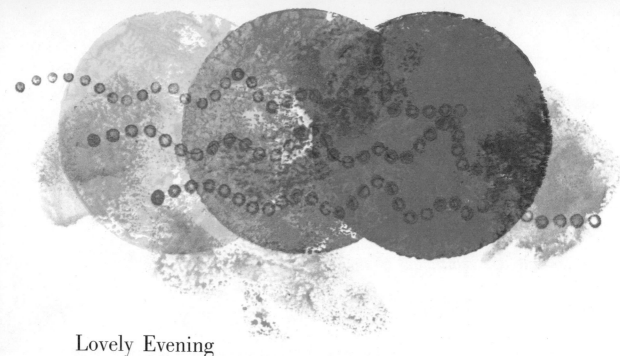

Lovely Evening

Traditional Round

You have discovered that singing in **thirds** creates pleasing harmony. Sing "Lovely Evening" as a round. Notice that when you sing phrases one and two at the same time, your voices are sounding in thirds.

1. Oh, how love - ly is the eve - ning, is the eve - ning,

2. When the bells are sweet - ly ring - ing, sweet - ly ring - ing.

3. Ding, dong, ding, dong, ding, dong.

Gladness

Swedish-German Round
Words by Max Exner

Glad - ness costs you not a thing,

And he who's hap - py is a king.

Sing "Gladness" as a four-part round. Enjoy the sound of the harmony. When you sing all four measures at the same time, you are singing **chords.**

Put the last note of each measure on a staff, one above the other. How many different pitches do you find? What is the **interval** between the lowest pitch and the middle pitch? What is the interval between the middle pitch and the highest pitch?

When "piled up" thirds are sounded together, we hear a **chord.** Here are the chords you heard when you sang "Gladness" as a round.

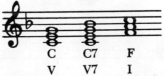

Play the chords on the autoharp and on the bells. Study the chords and answer these questions.

Which pitches are used in each chord?

What steps of the scale are used in each chord?

Why are the chords named C, C7, F?

Why are they named V, V7, I?

Little Fox

English Folk Song

1. Lit - tle fox went out on a chil - ly night;
2. So the fox he ran till he came to the pen;

He prayed to the moon to give him light.
The ducks and the geese were put there - in.

He'd man - y a mile to go that night
"A cou - ple of you will grease my chin

Be - fore he'd reach the town - o, town - o, town - o,
Be - fore I leave this town - o, town - o, town - o,

He'd man - y a mile to go that night
A cou - ple of you will grease my chin

Be - fore he'd reach the town - o.
Be - fore I leave this town - o."

3. Well he grabbed a grey goose by the neck;
   He flung it up across his back.
   He didn't mind the quack, quack, quack,
   And the legs all dangling down-o   } 2 times

4. Now old Missus Flipperflopper jumped out of bed;
   And up to the window she cocked her head.
   She cried, "John, O John, the grey goose is gone,
   And the fox is on the town-o."   } 2 times

5. Little fox he ran till he came to his den;
   And there were his little ones, eight, nine, ten.
   They said, "Daddy, you'd better go back again,
   It must be a mighty fine town-o."   } 2 times

This song can be accompanied on the autoharp using the chords you found when you studied "Gladness."

Look at the melody. Find patterns with tones that belong to the F chord. Play that chord on the autoharp with those measures.

Find patterns with tones that belong to the C7 chord. Play that chord with those measures.

You will find some measures that need a third chord. It is made up of these tones. Can you decide what it should be named?

When you have selected chords for each measure, accompany the song on the autoharp. Did you choose the right chords? Your ears will help you decide.

Virginia Reel

Early American Folk Dance

The **reel** was originally danced in England to the music of an Irish jig. It was brought to our country by the early settlers and was a popular dance of pioneer Americans.

The reel was danced to many different tunes. "Turkey in the Straw," the tune played on your recording, was one of the favorites. Listen to the dance tune played on the violin, clarinet, accordion, banjo, and double bass.

Listen to the music to discover when to begin the dance again with a new head couple. You will dance these patterns used in many early American dances.

Forward and back
Right hand around
Left hand around
Both hands around
Do-si-do
Sashay down and back
Reel the set and sashay back
Cast off to the foot
Form an arch
Form a new set

Other Arts of Long Ago

You have been learning music of long ago. You have discovered that the music of earlier times is similar to the music of our time in some ways and different in others. You have discovered that learning music of long ago helps you imagine life of that time.

Other arts also help us understand the people of long ago. As we enjoy the paintings, sculpture, and poetry of earlier times, we can learn about the activities of the people and the ideas they found important.

My flowers shall not perish
Nor shall my chants cease
They spread, they scatter.

—Aztec (Mexico)

Throughout the world
Who is there like little me!
Who is like me!
I can touch the sky,
I touch the sky indeed!

—Winnebago (North America)

A Prayer

of the Havasupai (North America)

Sun, my relative
Be good coming out
Do something good for us.

Make me work,
So I can do anything in the garden
I hoe, I plant corn, I irrigate.

You, sun, be good going down at sunset
We lay down to sleep I want to feel good.

While I sleep you come up.
Go on your course many times.
Make good things for us men.

Make me always the same as I am now.

My arms, they wave high in the air,
My hands, they flutter behind my back; they
    wave above my head like the wings
    of a bird.
Let me move my face, let me dance, let me
    shrug my shoulders, let me shake my body.
Let me fold my arms, let me crouch down,
Let me hold my hands under my chin.

—Eskimo (Arctic)

From "The Indians' Book" by Natalie Curtis, copyright 1907, 1923, and renewed in 1950 by Dover Publications, Inc., New York. Reprinted by permission.

Sleep brings pearl necklaces, do not cry, baby,
Sleep brings sweet dishes, do not cry, baby,
Do not cry, baby,
It is time, you must sleep now,
As the fish sleeps in the pool.

—Mikiris (India)

O Sun, O Sun
Death comes, the end arrives,
The tree falls and dies.
O Sun, O Sun,
The child is born in his mother's womb.
Death saw, man saw, the Sun saw.
Sun, O Sun, O Sun.

—Gabon Pygmie (Africa)

Study the art objects on these two pages. Some were created over a thousand years ago. Others are only a few hundred years old. What activity did the people of these different times enjoy that we still enjoy today?

Flautista e Citarista
Etruscan fresco from Tomb of Leopards, Tarquinia

Lautenengel (Angel playing the lute)
by Hans Brüggeman

Dioskòurides of Samos:
Street Musicians

Herculaneum mosaic,
Nazionale, Naples

Pottery Girls on a Swing,
Forming Whistles
Vera Cruz, Mexico

117

The Family
by Charles Alston

Music Here and Now

You have learned songs of far away and of long ago. One of the wonderful things about the time in which we live is that we can enjoy the music and other arts of different times and places. We can hear the music on recordings and at concerts. We can enjoy other arts in museums and in books.

In this unit you will discover that some music written by composers of today is similar to the music of long ago. You will discover that some music of today sounds very different from the music of long ago.

As you explore the new music and other arts of today, compare them with examples from long ago and far away. Are the ideas and feelings expressed similar or different? What differences do you discover in the use of materials or in the way the artists organize their ideas?

Experiment with composing new music of your own. Create new art of your own. Express the feelings and ideas of the time in which you live.

Happiness

Words and Music by Clark Gesner

This song is from a musical comedy, "You're a Good Man, Charlie Brown." Musical comedy was developed by American composers of this century. Very often it tells a story through words, music, and dramatization.

Broadly

1. Hap- pi - ness   is   two kinds of ice   cream,
2. Hap- pi - ness   is   five dif - f'rent cray - ons,

Find - ing your skate key,   tell - ing the   time.
Know- ing a   se - cret, climb- ing a   tree.

(1). Hap - pi - ness   is   learn - ing to   whis - tle,
(2.) Hap - pi - ness   is   find - ing a   nick - el,
(3.) Hap - pi - ness   is   hav - ing a   sis - ter,

Ty - ing your shoes for the   ver - y   first time.
Catch- ing a   fire - fly, ___ set - ting him free.
Shar - ing a   sand - wich, ___ get - ting a - long.

120

Hap-pi-ness is play-ing the drum in your own school band.
Hap-pi-ness is be-ing a-lone ev-ery now and then.
Hap-pi-ness is sing-ing to-geth-er when day is through.

1.

And Hap-pi-ness is walk-ing hand in (1.) hand. _____
And Hap-pi-ness is com-ing home a-
And Hap-pi-ness is those who sing with

2. & 3.

(2.) gain. _____
(3.) you. _____ } (2. & 3.) Hap-pi-ness is morn-ing and eve-ning,

Day - time and night - time too,

For Hap-pi-ness is an-y-one, and an-y-thing at all

Optional: repeat from 𝄋 to Fine.

That's loved by you. _____

Fine

From the musical play YOU'RE A GOOD MAN, CHARLIE BROWN, music and lyrics by
Clark Gesner, © 1965, 1967 by JEREMY MUSIC, INC. All rights reserved.
Reprinted by permission.

Ionisation

by Edgar Varèse

Listen to "Ionisation." Discuss reasons why you know that this was composed by a composer of today rather than by a composer of long ago.

After you have discussed your reasons, listen again and try to identify the instruments you hear. Some which are heard are not usually considered musical instruments. What do you think Varèse used to produce the low, wailing sound?

Notice how sounds of contrasting quality are heard one after the other. Booming, ringing, swishing, and rattling sounds quickly follow one another. High-pitched sounds follow low-pitched sounds. Loud sections are contrasted with calmer, quieter sections.

Listen for a **climax**, that is, an important point in the music. How does the composer organize his sounds to create this important point? Do you hear any repetitions of patterns?

Ionization is a scientific word which means, "the adding or subtracting of one or more electrons to an atom, giving it an electrical charge." Why do you think Varèse chose this title for his composition?

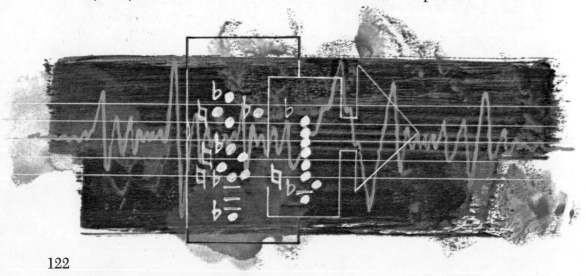

Music of Your Own

Composers of today often write music for unusual instruments. They may write their music in new ways. Here are four short compositions, each to be played on a tambourine. Study the musical scores. Decide what the different signs mean. Perform the compositions.

Look for an object in your home or classroom which makes an interesting sound. Experiment with your new "instrument." How many different kinds of sounds can you produce on it?

Create a composition for your new instrument. Can you write your new music so that someone else can perform it?

How Does My Lady's Garden Grow?

Music by Arthur Frackenpohl
Words from Mother Goose

The composers of the songs on this page and the next live in the United States today. Compare the sounds of the two songs. Could either have been composed long ago?

A Timely Rhyme

Music by Jean Moe
Words Anonymous

Play the scale on which this song is based. Play the melody pattern for "I see in what." Do these tones belong to the scale you played first? This pattern is based on a **whole tone scale.**

Play these two scales. Why is "whole tone" a good name for them?

Find other patterns in the song that are based on this scale. Find patterns that are from the F major scale.

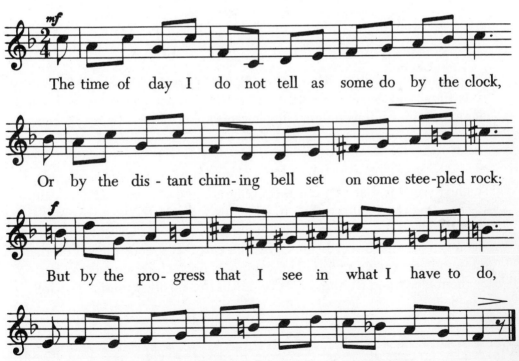

The time of day I do not tell as some do by the clock,

Or by the dis - tant chim - ing bell set on some stee - pled rock;

But by the pro - gress that I see in what I have to do,

It's ei - ther "done o'- clock" for me, or on - ly "half - past through."

Petrouchka Ballet Suite

Scene One, "The Shrovetide Fair"

by Igor Stravinsky

This music was written for a **ballet**. Ballet is a stage dance performed in costume and accompanied by music. The ballet dancer must learn many patterns of movement. The **choreographer** plans a ballet by combining the movements in many ways.

The main character of this ballet is a clown puppet named Petrouchka. The first scene is that of a fair in Leningrad. We see the dancers in the stage setting representing the crowd at the fair. On the stage are stalls, sideshows, and the showman's small wooden stage with closed curtains. The music of merriment begins with the carnival sounds played on the flutes and other instruments. The composer uses a folk song as the basis for the melody and rhythm he develops in the carnival music. The folk song begins.

(sounds an octave higher)

The crowd mingles happily, hearing the music from the different booths. A man plays a hand organ as a girl dances for pennies. The composer based his music on a tune which he once heard an organ grinder play.

(sounds an octave higher)

The orchestra plays the first section of the music again while the dancers continue to dramatize the merriment of the crowd.

Suddenly the showman draws the curtain and we see his puppets: the Ballerina, a doll with red cheeks; the Moor, a big, dark fellow; and floppy Petrouchka. The showman plays his flute as he introduces the puppets. As he touches them, the puppets spring to life. When all three are in motion, they dance together in a wild Russian dance.

(sounds an octave higher)

The Crow

Music by Igor Stravinsky
Words by Linda Rosenbloom

This song was written by the composer of "Petrouchka." Listen to the recording of the song. Is this music in any way similar to music of long ago?

On a bridge a- bove the bay Sat a crow one sun-ny day.

I took him by the tail and heel, Then up-on the bridge I _ kneel'd.

In the bay I set him To watch the wa-ter wet him.

Next day I came back to see, Un-der- neath the bridge was he.

I took him out and with a sigh, Put him in the sun to _ dry.

Yes-ter-day I saw him; The sun's still shin-ing on him.

Psalm 100

Music by Jane M. Marshall

The words of this song are ancient. The music was composed by a composer of today.

Make a joy - ful noise un - to the Lord, all ye lands.

Serve the Lord with glad - ness: come be - fore his pres - ence with

sing - ing.   En - ter his gates with thanks-giv - ing,

and his courts, his courts with praise:

Make a joy - ful noise un - to the Lord,

all   ye   lands.

Brethren in Peace Together

Jewish Folk Song
Paraphrase of Psalm 133:1

Look at the key signature. On what scale is this song based? Look at the
notes. Play them from low to high. Does the pattern sound like the scale
you named?

How good - ly it is and how pleas - ant,

for breth - ren to dwell to - geth - er.

1. How good - ly it is and how pleas - ant,

for breth - ren to dwell to - geth - er.

2. Good - ly, pleas - ant, Breth-ren in peace to - geth - er.

How good - ly it is and how pleas - ant,

for breth - ren to dwell to - geth - er.

This Train

American Folk Song

Chant, "This train is bound for glory." Tap the pattern you chanted. Which word did you hold longer, "This," or "train"?

Listen to the recording. Is the rhythm sung the same way you chanted it? The rhythm you hear in "This Train" is called **syncopation.**

1. This train is bound for glo - ry, This train, __
2. This train don't pull no ex - tras, This train, __

This train is bound for glo - ry, This train, __
This train don't pull no ex - tras, This train, __

This train is bound for glo - ry,
This train don't pull no ex - tras,

Don't ride noth - in' but the good and ho - ly,
Don't pull noth - in' but the mid - night spe - cial,

This train is bound for glo - ry, This train! __
This train don't pull no ex - tras, This train! __

Marching to Pretoria

South African Folk Melody
Words by Josef Marais

Look at the meter signature. How will the rhythm move? What note will sound with the beat? If you are not sure, listen to the recording and tap the beat. What word patterns sound with the beat? What kind of note is used for these words?

How will the quarter note sound in relation to the beat?

How will the dotted quarter note sound in relation to the eighth note?

If you are still not sure, practice these patterns.

I'm with you and you're with me, And so we are all to-geth-er, So we are all to-geth-er, So we are

132

all to-geth-er. Sing with me, I'll sing with you, And so we will

sing to-geth-er As we march a - long.___

Refrain

We are march-ing to Pre - to - ri - a,___

Pre - to - ri - a,___ Pre - to - ri - a,___

___ We are march-ing to Pre - to - ri - a,___

Pre - to - ri - a, hur - rah!___

133

Banana Boat
Loader's Song

Jamaican Folk Song

This song from the West Indies is a **calypso** work song. Find the West Indies on a map.

Day oh! Day— oh! Day is break - ing,— I wan' go home.—

1. Come, Mis - ter Tal - ly - man, come tal - ly   my ba - nan - as.
2. Came here for work, I   did - n't come here for to   i - dle.

Day   is   break - ing, ___   I   wan'   go   home. ___

3. Three han', four han', five han', Bunch!

Six   han', seven han', eight han', Bunch!

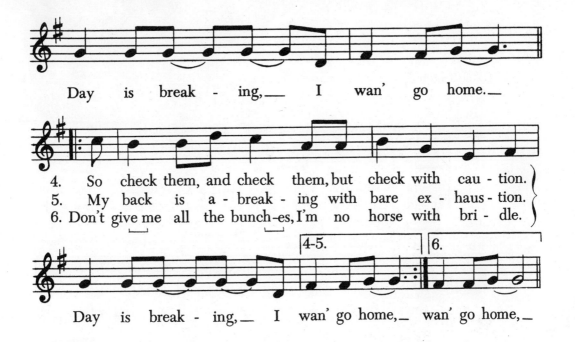

Day   is   break - ing, ___   I   wan'   go   home. ___

4.   So   check them, and check   them, but   check with   cau - tion.
5.   My   back   is   a - break - ing with   bare   ex - haus - tion.
6. Don't give me   all   the bunch-es, I'm   no   horse with   bri - dle.

|4-5.   **|6.**

Day   is   break - ing, ___   I   wan' go home, ___   wan' go home, ___

People from the West Indies often improvise percussion accompaniments for their songs. They use deep-pitched **conga drums**, two-headed **bongo drums**, and **cowbells**. They also play **maracas**, which are gourds filled with dried seeds. **Claves**, sticks made of hardwood, always have had an important part in accompaniments from the West Indies.

Find these patterns in the song. Practice each pattern until you can play it correctly. When the class knows all the patterns, choose the ones that you like best to accompany the song.

Tafta Hindy

Old Arabic Song

Brightly

1. "Taf - ta Hin - dy, Taf - ta Hin - dy," Who will buy my
2. "Taf - ta Hin - dy, Taf - ta Hin - dy," Come a - long and

clothes to __ wear? Silks and sat - ins, love - ly lac - es,
join the __ fun. Lit - tle trin - kets, col - ored rib - bons,

gold and sil - ver for your hair, Silks and sat - ins,
there's e - nough for ev - ery - one, Lit - tle trin - kets,

love - ly lac - es, gold and sil - ver for your __ hair.
col - ored rib - bons, there's e - nough for ev - ery - one.

Play this accompaniment on the bells as the class sings the song.

Someone else may make up a rhythm part to play on the tambourine.

136

Zum Gali Gali

Israeli Work Song

People take the music of other lands and make it their own. In Israel,
this is a work song. In the United States, we sing it for recreation.

1. He - cha - lutz   l' - maan a - vo - dah; ____
2. A - vo - dah   l' - maan he - cha - lutz; ____
3. He - cha - lutz   l' - maan ha - b'tu - lah; ____
4. Ha - sha - lom   l' - maan ha - 'a - mim; ____

Chant

Zum   ga - li ga - li ga - li, Zum ga - li ga - li,

___ A - vo - dah   l' - maan he - cha - lutz.
___ He - cha - lutz   l' - maan a - vo - dah.
___ Ha - b'tu - lah   l' - maan he - cha - lutz.
___ Ha - 'a - mim   l' - maan ha - sha - lom.

Zum   ga - li ga - li ga - li, Zum ga - li ga - li.

Sing the chant softly as an **introduction** to the song. At the end of the
fourth verse, repeat the chant several times as a **coda**. Let your voices
grow gradually softer in a **diminuendo**. Gradually sing more slowly
during the last repetition in a **ritard**.

137

Doney Gal

Cowboy Song

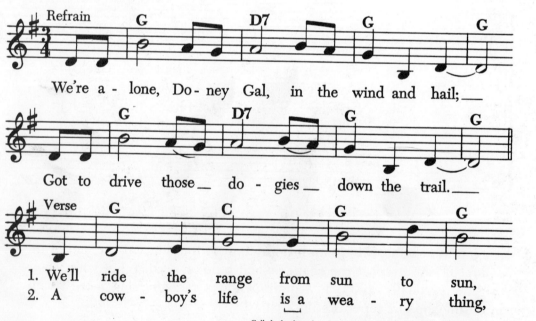

Refrain

We're a-lone, Do-ney Gal, in the wind and hail; __

Got to drive those __ do-gies __ down the trail. __

Verse

1. We'll ride the range from sun to sun,
2. A cow-boy's life is a wea-ry thing,

Colledted, adapted, and arranged by John A. Lomax and Alan Lomax.
Copyright 1938 by Ludlow Music, Inc., New York, N.Y. Reprinted by permission.

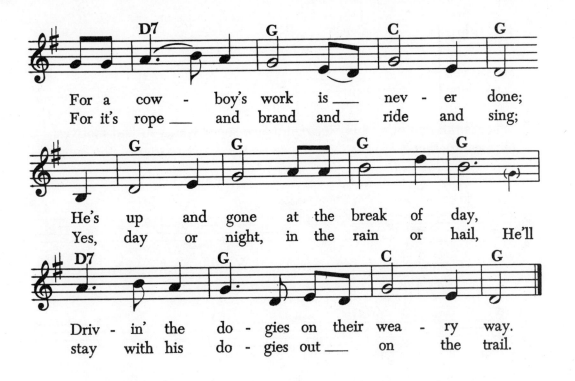

For a cow - boy's work is ___ nev - er done;
For it's rope ___ and brand and ___ ride and sing;

He's up and gone at the break of day,
Yes, day or night, in the rain or hail, He'll

Driv - in' the do - gies on their wea - ry way.
stay with his do - gies out ___ on the trail.

Accompaniments to cowboy songs often suggest an "on the trail" feeling. On the recording this feeling is provided by the guitar and temple blocks. Listen to the recording and develop a similar accompaniment of your own. On the piano, play a pattern similar to the one you heard on the guitar.

Sometimes you will have to change one note in the pattern to create better harmony with the melody.

Decide when you will play pattern A and when pattern B.

La Jesucita

Mexican Folk Song
English Words Adapted

What is the design of this Mexican dance song? Can you find **motives, phrases, sections?** Plan a dance that matches the design of the song.

Come let us dance where the lan-terns shine bright-ly, _____
Va - mos al bai - ley ve - rás ¡qué bo - ni - to! _____

Come let us join in the fun step-ping light-ly. ___
don - de se a - lum - bran con vein - te lin - ter - nas, ___

Down in the square where the danc - ers are swing-ing _____
don - de se bai - lan las dan - zas mo - der - nas, _____

And all the lat - est of steps can be seen. Tra la la la!
don - de se bai - la de mu-cho va - ci - lón. Ya - ya - ya - ya!

Oh, dance with me, Je - su - si - ta,
Y quié - re - me, Je - su - si - ta,

Oh, please, won't you dance with me?
y quié - re - me por fa - vor.

If you'll be my danc - ing part - ner,
Y mi - ra que soy tu a - man - te,

Then your faith - ful slave I'll be.
y se - gu - ro ser - vi - dor.

Old Songs in New Packages

People enjoy singing old songs. Often musicians make **arrangements** of old songs by changing the melodies and rhythms, adding harmony, or composing accompaniments. These arrangements make the songs sound new.

Listen to "Las mananitas" sung by a popular singing group from Mexico. You learned this song on page 12. Does this arrangement sound like the song you learned? How has it been changed?

Notice that the accompaniment is played by a **mariachi band.** Can you identify the instruments you hear? Mariachi bands are often heard in Mexico and in the southwest part of the United States.

Now listen to an arrangement of another old song. This is the gospel song, "This Little Light of Mine." It has been a favorite religious song of many people. How do you know that this is a new arrangement? What instruments accompany the soloist and chorus? This song is in your book on page 142. Learn to sing the song as it is written in your book.

141

This Little Light of Mine

Spiritual
Arranged by Buryl A. Red

Ev - ery way, Yes, ev - ery

way, Yes, ev - ery

day, I'm __ a - gon - na let my lit - tle light

shine, let it shine! __

America, the Beautiful

Music by Samuel A. Ward
Words by Katharine Lee Bates

1. O beau - ti - ful for spa - cious skies,
2. O beau - ti - ful for pil - grim feet
3. O beau - ti - ful for he - roes proved

For am - ber waves of grain,
Whose stern, im - pas - sioned stress
In lib - er - at - ing strife,

For pur - ple moun - tain maj - es - ties
A thor - ough - fare for free - dom beat
Who more than self their coun - try loved,

A - bove the fruit - ed plain!
A - cross the wil - der - ness!
And mer - cy more than life!

A - mer - i - ca, A - mer - i - ca,
A - mer - i - ca, A - mer - i - ca,
A - mer - i - ca, A - mer - i - ca,

God   shed   his   grace   on   thee,
God   mend   thine   ev - ery   flaw,
May   God   thy   gold   re - fine,

And   crown   thy   good   with   broth - er - hood
Con - firm   thy   soul   in   self - con - trol,
Till   all   suc - cess   be   no - ble - ness,

From   sea   to   shin - ing   sea.
Thy   lib - er - ty   in   law.
And   ev - ery   gain   di - vine.

The Upward Trail

Traditional Words and Music

We're on the up - ward trail, we're on the up - ward trail,

Sing - ing, sing - ing, ev - ery - bod - y sing - ing, as we go.

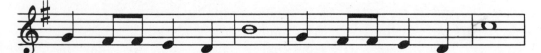

We're on the up - ward trail, we're on the up - ward trail,

Sing - ing, sing - ing, ev - ery - bod - y sing - ing, home - ward bound.

146

Make New Friends

Traditional Round

Although the round is a very old form of music, we still enjoy singing rounds today.

Make new friends, but keep the old;

One is sil - ver and the oth - er gold.

French Cathedrals

Traditional French Round

Or - lé - ans, Beau - gen - cy, No - tre Dame

de Clé - ry, Ven - dô - me, Ven - dô - me.

147

It's Quiet on the Moon

Words and Music
by Ruth De Cesare

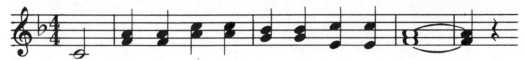

It's   qui - et   on   the shin - ing moon to - night;___
Per - haps we'll reach the shin - ing moon to - night;___

Fine

We've   seen its pic - ture   from   our   sat - el - lite.___

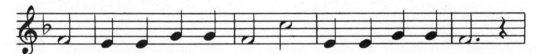

Now   all   the   stars are wink - ing,   bright-en - ing   the   sky;

D.C. al Fine

Lone - ly   plan - ets   blink - ing   show   it's   time   to   try.

Bowery Bum
by Jean Dubuffet

Bowery Bum

Study after Jean Dubuffet
by Ilhan Mimaroglu

The composer of "Bowery Bum" got the idea for the composition from a drawing of the same name. The artist had used one material, India ink, for his visual composition. The composer limited himself to one sound source, or "instrument," for his musical composition.

Listen to the recording. Can you identify the sound source that is used? Remember, all the sounds you hear came originally from the same source.

The source for all the different sounds is a single rubber band! The sound of the rubber band being plucked and snapped was recorded on tape. These sounds were then altered and combined in various ways to create the actual composition. This is electronic music. Listen again. Does it now seem that the music could all have come from one rubber band?

As you listen a third time, study the drawing at the top of the page. In what other ways does the music reflect the feelings and ideas suggested by the picture?

149

The Dancers, by Edgar Degas

Artists get ideas for their works from many sources. They respond to the people around them, to important events, to the world of nature. Sometimes they are inspired by other arts.

Look at the painting on this page. What art inspired Dégas to paint this picture? On page 152 a poet expressed ideas inspired by the same art.

Look through your book. Can you find musical examples that were composed in response to visual arts? Can you find visual art that was inspired by music?

Forsythia

by Mary Ellen Solt

"Forsythia" is an example of **concrete poetry**. The way it looks is as important as the words in helping us understand the poet's ideas.

You have enjoyed works of art that were inspired by a different art. Create art of your own that expresses what you discover in another art form.

Compose instrumental music inspired by the poem, "Forsythia."

Paint a picture that reflects your experience in listening to *Symphony No. 11* or *Quartet in C Major.*

Dance as someone reads the excerpt from "chanson innocent."

Choose one of the paintings in your book. Write a poem that expresses in words what you see in the painting.

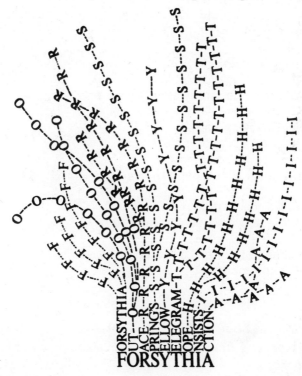

151

Lines Written for Gene Kelly to Dance to

by Carl Sandburg

Spring is when the grass turns green and glad.
Spring is when the new grass comes up and says, "Hey, hey! Hey, hey!"
Be dizzy now and turn your head upside down and see how
    the world looks upside down.
Be dizzy now and turn a cartwheel, and see the good earth
    through a cartwheel.

Tell your feet the alphabet.
Tell your feet the multiplication table.
Tell your feet where to go, and watch 'em go and come back.

Can you dance a question mark?
Can you dance an exclamation point?
Can you dance a couple of commas?
And bring it to a finish with a period?

Can you dance like the wind is pushing you?
Can you dance like you are pushing the wind?
Can you dance with slow wooden heels
    and then change to bright and singing silver heels?
Such nice feet, such good feet.

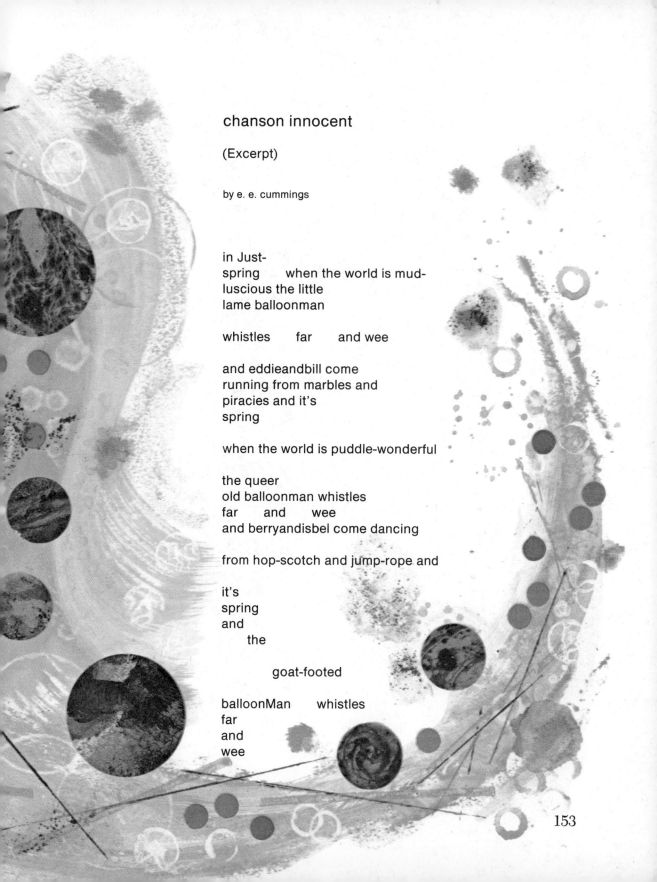

chanson innocent

(Excerpt)

by e. e. cummings

in Just-
spring   when the world is mud-
luscious the little
lame balloonman

whistles   far   and wee

and eddieandbill come
running from marbles and
piracies and it's
spring

when the world is puddle-wonderful

the queer
old balloonman whistles
far   and   wee
and berryandisbel come dancing

from hop-scotch and jump-rope and

it's
spring
and
    the

        goat-footed

balloonMan   whistles
far
and
wee

Koshare Rainbow Dance
by Awah Tsireh

More Music to Explore

As you explore more music, try to put to use all that you have learned this year. What do you know about the songs of long ago, far away, and here and now? What do the songs have in common? How are they different?

What do you know about music of composers of long ago, far away, and here and now? Review some of their compositions.

What have you discovered about other arts? Discuss what the different arts have in common with music.

What have you learned about rhythm, melody, harmony, and design in music? What can you do by yourself? Can you learn a new melody, plan an accompaniment, make up a composition of your own?

What important words have you learned to use when you speak of music? Make a list of important words found in your book. Use these words when you want to tell others what you hear and see in music.

Use all your knowledge as you continue to explore music and other arts of far away, long ago, and here and now.

Yellow Submarine

Words and Music
by John Lennon and Paul McCartney

Is this a song of long ago, far away, or here and now? What helps you
to know? Find the design. How will knowing the design help you learn
the song?

March tempo

In the town ___ where I was born lived a

man ___ who sailed to sea, And he told ___ us of his

life in the land ___ of sub - ma -

rines. So we sailed ___ up to the sun till we

found ___ the sea of green. And we lived ___ be- neath the

waves in our yel - low sub - ma - rine.

Chorus

We all live in a yel - low sub - ma - rine,

yel - low sub - ma - rine, yel - low sub - ma - rine,

We all live in a yel - low sub - ma - rine,

yel - low sub - ma - rine, yel - low sub - ma - rine. { And our
                                                      As we

friends__ are all on board, man - y more of them __ live next
live__ a life of ease, ev - ery one of us__ has all we

1.
door. And the band__ be - gins to play . . .
need: Sky of blue __ and sea of

2.   *Repeat Chorus from the 𝄋 and fade.*
green, in our yel - low sub - ma - rine.

Swing Low, Sweet Chariot

Spiritual
Arranged by William S. Haynie

Swing low, sweet char - i - ot, __ Com - ing for to car - ry me home,

Swing low, sweet char - i - ot, __ Com - ing for to car - ry me home.

1. I looked o - ver Jor - dan and what did I see? __
2. If you get __ there __ be - fore __ I do, __
3. I'm some - times __ up __ and some - times down, __

A band_ of an - gels
Just tell__ my friends I'm
But still__ my soul feels

Com - ing for to car - ry me home.

com - ing af - ter me,____
com - ing___ too,____
heav - en - ly___ bound.__

Com - ing for to car - ry me home.

All night, all ___ day, An - gels watch-ing o - ver

Swing low, sweet char - i - ot, ___ Com-ing for to car - ry me

me, My Lord, ___ All night, all _____ day,

home, Swing - low, sweet char - i - ot, ___

An - gels watch - ing o - ver me. me.

Com - ing for to car - ry me home. home.

Ua Nani O Nu'uanu

Traditional Hawaiian Stick Dance

This is a modern version of an ancient hula kala'au or stick dance. Look at the music. What does this song have in common with other ancient songs you have learned?

1. U - a na - ni o Nu - 'u - a - nu
   i ka la - u o ke Ka - we - lu.

2. U - a ha - la - wai a - ku - la
   me ka ma - ka - ni nu - i.

3. E 'i - 'i - ni a - na ka ma - na - 'o
   E i - ke ia___ Ka - hu - ai - la - na.

160

4. O ko - 'u hoa no i - a

o ka U - a ___ Ki - o - wa - o. **2**

5. U - a po - no no ka - u - a

Ho - 'o - ko - hu a - na ka ma - na - 'o. **2**

6. Ha - 'i - na mai ka i - no - a

o ka la - ni 'I - o - la - ni. **2**

Follow Me

Traditional Carol

This two-part song uses an ancient form known as **canon**. Study the song. Make a definition for "canon." Why is "Follow Me" a good title for a song that is a canon?

Study the rhythm. Notice the many rests. Do you know how long to be silent when you see each rest? To help you decide, divide into two groups and tap these patterns.

Make up your own percussion canon. One person begins by playing a pattern on an instrument of his choice. Another person echoes him on another instrument. The leader may begin again before his echo has completed the pattern. The echo player must listen carefully to be sure he repeats exactly what the leader played.

Dakota Hymn

American Indian Melody
Words Paraphrased by William Frazier

Here is another song of long ago. On what kind of scale is the melody based? To help you decide, locate all the different pitches that are used in the song. Play them on the bells from low to high.

1. Man - y and great, O God, are thy things,
2. Grant un - to us com - mun - ion with thee,

Mak - er of earth and sky. Thy hands have set the
Thou star - a - bid - ing one; Come un - to us and

heav - ens with stars, Thy fin - gers spread the
dwell with ___ us; With thee are found the

moun - tains and plains. Lo, at thy word the
gifts of ___ life. Bless us with life that

wa - ters were formed; Deep seas o - bey thy voice.
has no ___ end, E - ter - nal life with thee.

164

Bound for the Rio Grande

Sea Chantey

1. Oh, say were you ev - er in Ri - o Grande?
2. And good-bye, fare ye well, all you la - dies of town,
3. So it's pack up your don - key and get un - der way,

It's there that the riv - er flows
Oh, _____ Ri - o. ___ We'll see you a - gain when our
We'll head for the South where they'll

down gold - en sand.
trip is full round. } And we're bound for the Ri - o Grande.
give us more pay.

Refrain

Then a - way, love, ___ a - way. Way ___ down Ri - o, ___

So fare ___ ye well ___ my pret - ty young gel,

For we're bound for the Ri - o Grande. ___

Trouble in Mind

Spiritual

We have learned songs that express many ideas and are used for many different purposes. Sometimes songs such as this one help us express feelings we wouldn't say in any other way.

1. Trou - ble in mind, I'm blue,___ But I won't be blue al - ways, 'Cause the sun's gon-na shine ___ In my back - door some day.___

2. I'm all a - lone at mid - night, And my lamp is burn - ing low.___ I nev - er

3. I'm gon - na lay my head ___ On that lone - some rail - road line,___ And let that

166

had   so much trou-ble____ In __ my life be - fore. ____
two nine-teen _____ Pac - i - fy my mind. ____

Six Pieces for Orchestra, Opus 6

Third Piece

by Anton Webern

The particular sound of an instrument or a voice is its "tone color." Just as you can recognize a friend by the sound of his voice, you can recognize an instrument by its distinctive tone color.

Listen to this short piece by Webern. Why do you suppose his music is sometimes described as tone-color music? Suggest words which describe the tone colors in this short piece. Here is a chart showing Webern's use of instruments in the composition. Listen again as you watch the chart.

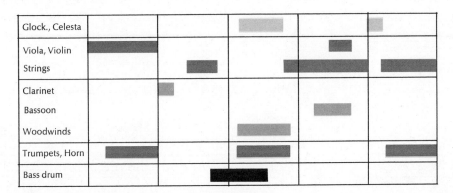

Although Webern wrote this piece for an entire orchestra, you seldom hear all of the instruments play at once. Listen as they pass melody patterns back and forth. Notice how the music covers a wide **range** from high to low as melodies pass from one instrument to another.

Usually when we describe design in music, we describe the sequence of same and different melodies. What helps create a design in Webern's music?

Let's Explore Tone Color

Look at the pictures of instruments found on the following pages. How many of them can you recognize by their sound? It is possible to identify an instrument by its sound because each has its own **tone color**.

When a composer writes an instrumental composition, he chooses certain instruments because of their distinctive tone color. He puts them together in different combinations to produce the special effect he wants us to hear.

Sometimes a composer writes a composition for full orchestra. Listen again to the "Háry János Suite" on page 64. How many of the instruments pictured on the following pages can you hear in this music?

Sometimes a composer writes for a small group of instruments. Locate the pictures of the instruments Mozart used for his composition discussed on page 108.

The instruments of the orchestra are grouped in four families: **string, woodwind, brass,** and **percussion.** As you study the pictures on the following pages, discuss reasons why the instruments in each group belong to the same family.

STRING FAMILY

VIOLA

VIOLIN

CELLO

DOUBLE BASS

HARP

169

WOODWIND FAMILY

BASSOON

OBOE

CLARINET

TENOR SAXOPHONE

170

FLUTE

BRASS FAMILY

TRUMPET

FRENCH HORN

TUBA

TROMBONE

171

PERCUSSION FAMILY

CHIMES

TRAP SET

ORCHESTRA BELLS

172

TIMPANI

CELESTA

Violin Concerto in D Major, Opus 61

Third Movement

by Ludwig van Beethoven

Listen to this concerto for solo violin and orchestra written by a composer of long ago. Compare it with the twentieth-century music you studied on page 167.

Study the details of the Beethoven composition. There are three different themes. Each theme is played first by the solo violin.

Listen to the first section. How many times do you hear the A theme?

Can you tell when a new section is about to begin? Here is the B theme.

The mood of the C section is different from A or B. Can you describe the differences?

There are seven sections in the movement. Listen to the music again, and write the design with letters. In what ways is the design different from the design of Webern's music?

Lullaby

by Johannes Brahms

Johannes Brahms, the composer of "Lullaby" and "The Blacksmith,"
lived nearly a hundred years ago. Why do you think his music is still
enjoyed today?

Quietly

1. Lull- a - by and good night, With ros- es be - dight,
2. Lull- a - by and good night, Thy moth-er's de - light,

With down o - ver - spread Is ba - by's wee bed.
Bright an - gels be - side My dar - ling a - bide.

Lay thee down now and rest, May thy slum - bers be blest;
They will guard thee at rest, Thou shalt wake on my breast,

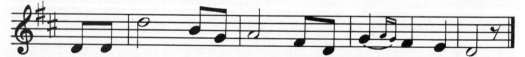

Lay thee down now and rest, May thy slum - bers be blest.
They will guard thee at rest, Thou shalt wake on my breast.

The Blacksmith

Music by Johannes Brahms
Words by William S. Haynie

Can you learn the rhythm of this song without help? Why will it be easy to learn?

Look at the key signature. Find home tone. Look at the melody. Why will phrase one be easy to sing?

Look at the last phrase. Notice the ♯ in measure three. Play C, then C ♯. Discuss the difference in sound. This sign ♮ tells us to sing C **natural** again in measure four.

1. The black-smith is strong, his stur-dy arm swing-ing,
2. The sparks fill the air, his ham-mer is pound-ing,

His ham-mer of steel on the an-vil is ring-ing,
And all through the vil-lage the rhy-thm is sound-ing.

With bang-ing and clang-ing it sounds all the day long.

175

Stodola Pumpa

Czechoslovakian Folk Melody
Words by A. D. Zanzig

1. Walk - ing at night a - long the mead - ow way,
2. Near - ing the wood, we heard the night - in - gale,

Home from the dance be - side my maid - en gay.
Sweet - ly it helped me tell my beg - ging tale.

Walk - ing at night a - long the mead - ow way,
Near - ing the wood, we heard the night - in - gale,

Home from the dance be - side my maid - en gay. *Hey!*
Sweet - ly it helped me tell my beg - ging tale. *Hey!*

Refrain

Sto - do - la, sto - do - la, sto - do - la pum - pa,

Sto - do - la pum - pa, sto - do - la pum - pa, pum, pum, pum.

176

The Roberts

Scottish Folk Dance

"The Roberts" is a favorite folk dance from Scotland. Listen to the dance music played on two accordions and a guitar.

This Scottish tune is divided into sections, each section 16 measures in length. You can dance the entire dance to each section of the music.

The dance is in the rhythm of the $\frac{6}{8}$ march with accents sounding two to a measure.

Form two circles for this dance, one inside the other. Each person faces a partner in the other circle. You will be doing the two-step, a foot pattern used in many dances. It is danced step-together-step. Practice the three foot patterns for "The Roberts."

step-slide, walk-walk-walk-walk
heel-toe, step-together-step
4 two-step patterns

Pretty Little Girl, Can You Answer Me?

Israeli Folk Song
English Text by Ruth Rubin

This is a song of far away. Do you know a song of long ago that is also a riddle song?

Oh, pret - ty lit - tle girl, Oh, can you an - swer me? Do you know the an - swers to my rid - dles, one, two, three?

1. What can grow ___
2. What falls down and
3. Where is the king with -

1. tall - er than a house? And what is ___
2. does - n't make a sound? What builds with - out
3. out ___ an - y land? And where is there

swift - er than _____ a mouse?
bricks up - on the bare ____ ground?
wa - ter with - out a grain of sand?

Sil - ly fel - low you, you are stu - pid

too, There's not a brain in - side your head, so

let me an - swer you:
1. Smoke
2. Snow, when it
3. The king of ____

ris - es tall - er than a house; A cat is ____
falls, ____ does - n't make a sound; Frost needs no
hearts, he has - n't an - y land; Tears from hu - man

swift - er than _____ a mouse.
bricks to build up - on the ground.
eyes ____ have - n't an - y sand.

Waltzing Matilda

Music by Marie Cowan
Words by A. B. Patterson

How much of this Australian song can you sing by yourself? Begin by practicing this pattern.

Then chant the words of the song in rhythm.

Locate home tone. Play 1 3 5. Look for patterns using these tones. Sing the song with numbers.

1. Once a jol - ly swag - man   camped_ by a bil - la - bong,
2. Down_ came a jum - buck to drink _ at the bil - la - bong,

Un - der the shade of a coo - li - bah tree,
Up jumped the swag - man, _ grabbed him with glee,

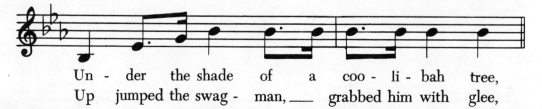

And he sang as he sat and wait - ed while his bil - ly boiled: ⎫
And he sang as he shoved that jum - buck in his tuck - er - bag: ⎭

Fine

"You'll come a - waltz - ing, Ma - til - da, with me."

"Waltz - ing Ma - til - da, waltz - ing Ma - til - da,

D.S. al Fine

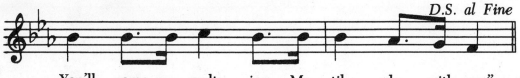

You'll come a - waltz - ing, Ma - til - da, with me."

3. Down came the squatter mounted on his thorobred,
   Up came the troopers, one, two, three,
   "Who's that jolly jumbuck you've got in your tucker-bag?
   You'll come a-waltzing, Matilda, with me."
   "Waltzing Matilda, waltzing Matilda,
   You'll come a-waltzing, Matilda, with me."
   "Who's that jolly jumbuck you've got in your tucker-bag?
   You'll come a-waltzing, Matilda, with me."

4. Up jumped the swagman, sprang into the billabong,
   "You'll never catch me alive!" said he.
   And his ghost may be heard as you pass by that billabong:
   "You'll come a-waltzing, Matilda, with me."
   "Waltzing Matilda, waltzing Matilda,
   You'll come a-waltzing, Matilda, with me."
   And his ghost may be heard as you pass by that billabong:
   "You'll come a-waltzing, Matilda, with me."

181

Pictures at an Exhibition

by Modest Mussorgsky

The Russian composer wrote this music to honor a friend who had been an architect and painter. The composer attended an exhibit of his sketches and paintings. Certain works of the artist became the subjects of the composer's musical "pictures."

Promenade

First the composer placed himself inside the gallery. As you listen to "Promenade," you will be able to imagine his walk through the art gallery. From the music, can you imagine what the composer looked like? The Promenade Theme is heard again before the musical description of several of the pictures.

The Tuileries

The gardens in Paris called the Tuileries are a favorite playground for children. The artist's picture represented a path in the garden with a group of children and nursemaids. The composer added his own title for the musical picture: "Dispute of the Children after Play." What musical ideas did the composer use to "paint" the picture in music?

Ballet of the Unhatched Chicks

The picture was a sketch for a child's ballet costume. The costume was supposed to make the dancer look like a chicken coming out of an egg. The composer looked at the costume sketch and imagined the child's dance. How does the music describe the dance and the "unhatched chicks"?

The Great Gate of Kiev

The architect's sketch showed a huge arched gate to be built in the city of Kiev. As the composer studied the sketch, he imagined a great procession. You will hear music describing military pageantry, chanting of priests, and triumphantly ringing bells. How did the composer relate this picture to the others and make it the **grand finale?**

When you know these "Pictures at an Exhibition," develop a dance for each composition. Connect your dances to make a complete dance-drama.

Later, turn to "Let's Explore Art," beginning on page 201. Attend your own exhibition of paintings and sculpture. You may wish to compose your own "Pictures at an Exhibition." Work in small groups; each group may compose music for a picture of its choice. As a class, compose a "promenade theme" which may be played between each "picture."

Allies Day, May 1917
by Childe Hassam

Music for Special Times

America for Me

Words and Music by
William S. Haynie

1. A - mer - i - ca, A - mer - i - ca, A land of hopes and
2. A - mer - i - ca, A - mer - i - ca, U - nit - ed may she

dreams. I love her moun-tains, fields and plains, Her
stand, From snow - capped peaks far in the North, To

for - ests and her streams. A na - tion where all
shores of sun and sand. Oh, may we ev - er

men are free, Where strength is built on in - dus - try, A -
faith - ful be, And guard the torch of lib - er - ty, A -

mer - i - ca, A - mer - i - ca, We pledge our hearts to thee.
mer - i - ca, A - mer - i - ca, A - mer - i - ca for me!

There Was an Old Witch

Traditional American Song

There was an old witch, Be - lieve it if you can,

She tapped on the win - dows and she ran, ran,_ ran.

She ran hel - ter - skel - ter with her toes in the air,

Corn - stalks fly - ing from the old witch -'s hair!

"Swish"_ goes the broom - stick, "Me - ow" goes the cat,

"Plop" goes the hop - toad Sit - ting on her hat.

"Whee," chuck - led I, "What fun! What fun!"

Hal - low - e'en night when the witch - es run.

Praise and Thanksgiving

Traditional Round

1. Praise and thanks - giv - ing let ev - ery one bring

2. Un - to our Fa - ther for ev - ery good thing.

3. All to - geth - er joy - ful - ly sing!

Come, Ye Thankful People, Come

Music by George J. Elvey
Words by Henry Alford

1. Come, ye thank-ful peo - ple, come, Raise the song of har-vest home;
2. All the world is God's own field, Fruit un - to his praise to yield;

All is safe - ly gath- ered in, Ere the win - ter storms be - gin;
Wheat and tares to- geth - er sown, Un - to joy or sor - row grown;

God, our Mak- er, doth pro - vide For our wants to be sup- plied;
First the blade, and then the ear, Then the full corn shall ap - pear;

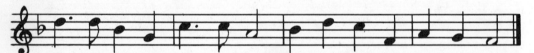

Come to God's own tem - ple, come, Raise the song of har-vest home.
Lord of har- vest, grant that we Whole-some grain and pure may be.

188

We Wish You a Merry Christmas

English Folk Song

We wish you a mer-ry Christ-mas, we wish you a mer-ry Christ-mas,

Fine

We wish you a mer-ry Christ-mas and a hap-py New Year.

Good tid-ings we bring for you and your kin:

Good tid-ings of Christ-mas and a hap-py New Year.

1. Now bring us some fig-gy pud-ding, now
2. We won't go un-til we get some, we

bring us some fig-gy pud-ding, Now
won't go un-til we get some, We

(after verse 2, D.C. al Fine)

bring us some fig-gy pud-ding, and bring some right here.
won't go un-til we get some, so bring some right here.

The Yodlers' Carol

Austrian Folk Melody
Arranged by Mary E. Caldwell
Words by Mary E. Caldwell

Descant

3. We have found lit - tle Je - sus, and we

1. From the snow - crowned moun - tain mead - ows, from the
2. Lit - tle stars shall be our can - dles as we
3. We have found him, lit - tle Je - sus, and we

kneel by his bed. The star o'er his

green wood - ed heights, We shall seek for the ___
jour - ney this night — Ti - ny dia - monds in the
kneel by his bed. See the bright star o'er his

cra - dle, how it crowns his head! We'll sing

man - ger on this calm, ho - ly night. Let's sing
heav - ens — we'll not want for a light. We sing
cra - dle; ra - diant light crowns his head! We'll sing

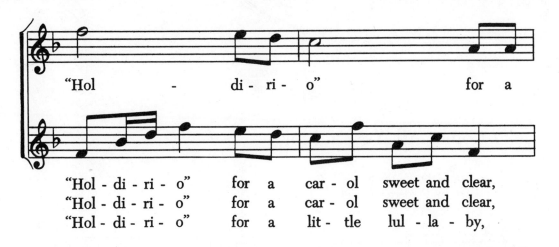

"Hol - di - ri - o" for a

"Hol - di - ri - o" for a car - ol sweet and clear,
"Hol - di - ri - o" for a car - ol sweet and clear,
"Hol - di - ri - o" for a lit - tle lul - la - by,

soft lul - la - by. Ah, _____

"Hol - di - ri - o" as on we go; Then comes "Hol - di - ri - o"
"Hol - di - ri - o" as on we go; Then comes "Hol - di - ri - o"
"Hol - di - ri - o" so soft and low. Now on tip - toe _ go,

not a sound, _____ home a - cross the snow. _

for an ech - o soft and clear, far a - cross the snow. _
for an ech - o soft and clear, far a - cross the snow. _
do not make a sin - gle sound; then home a - cross the snow. _

O Come, All Ye Faithful

Music from John F. Wade's "Cantus Diversi"
Translated by Frederick Oakeley

1. O come, all ye faith-ful, joy-ful and tri-um-phant,
2. Sing, choirs of an-gels, sing in ex-ul-ta-tion,

O come ye, O come ye to Beth-le-hem;
Sing, all ye cit-i-zens of heav'n a-bove!

Come and be-hold him, born the King of an-gels;
Glo-ry to God, all glo-ry in the high-est;

Refrain

O come, let us a-dore him, O come, let us a-dore him,

O come, let us a-dore him, Christ, the Lord!

Joseph Dearest, Joseph Mild

Old German Carol
Words Adapted

When you know the melody, the boys may sing the part of Joseph.
The girls may sing the part of Mary.

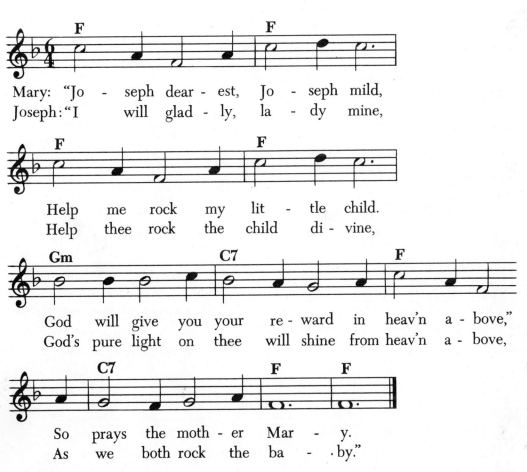

Mary: "Jo - seph dear - est, Jo - seph mild,
Joseph: "I will glad - ly, la - dy mine,

Help me rock my lit - tle child.
Help thee rock the child di - vine,

God will give you your re - ward in heav'n a - bove,"
God's pure light on thee will shine from heav'n a - bove,

So prays the moth - er Mar - y.
As we both rock the ba - by."

193

Jesus the Christ Is Born

Words and Music by John Jacob Niles

1. Je - sus the Christ is born,
2. Ye might - y kings of earth,

Give thanks now, ev - ery one.
Be - fore the man - ger bed,

Re - joice ye great ones and ye small,
Cast down, cast down your gold - en crown

God's will, it hath been done.
From off your roy - al head.

3. For in this lowly guise
   The Son of God doth sleep;
   And see the Queen of Heaven kneel,
   Her faithful vigil keep.

4. Two angels at His Head,
   Two angels at His feet;
   Beside His bed the flower red,
   Perfuming there so sweet.

5. Jesus the Christ is born,
   Give thanks now, every one.
   Rejoice ye great ones and ye small,
   God's will, it hath been done.

Arruru

Spanish Folk Melody
English Words by Elena Paz

1. Se - ño - ra do - ña Ma - rí - a,
2. The shep - herds are slow - ly wind - ing
3. A - blaze in the win - try sky, ____

I bring you my lit - tle one.
Their way from the dis - tant hills,
The dia - mond of Beth - le - hem,

He'll help you to rock the cra - dle,
To wit - ness the new - born Ba - by,
How bright is the star on high, ____

Where - in lies your new - born son.
They've braved all of win - ter's ills.
O - ver Je - ru - sa - lem.

Refrain

A - rru - ru, a - rru - ru,

Duer - me - te, Ni - ño Je - sús. sús.

Cuckoo Carol

Czechoslovakian Carol

Find the signs "*f*" and "*p*" above the staff of the refrain. These are marks of expression. Listen to the recording. What do these marks tell the singer to do?

Notice how these expression marks help to give the effect of an echo. Learn to play the echoes on the bells.

1. Walk-ing a - long the road,　I　bear a　hap-py load;
2. Wise Men who came from far,　Guid-ed　by　one bright star,

One　cuck-oo do I　to　the Christ Child take,
Bring　on their cam-els won-d'rous gifts for　you:

This　will a pret-ty pres-ent for him make,
Myrrh, frank-in-cense, and gold of shin-ing hue;

This　bring I　for his　sake.)
Glad　shep-herds came __　too.)

Refrain

Cuck-oo, Cuck-oo, Cuck-oo, Cuck-oo! Oh, from your bas-ket
Oh, Christ Child, like my

don't es - cape,
gift the best, ⎫
⎭ Cuck-oo, Cuck-oo, Cuck-oo, Cuck-oo!

Hap - py the Christ Child will a - wake,
Soft let your fin - gers on him rest,

Hap - py the Christ Child will a - wake.
Soft let your fin - gers on him rest.

All Beautiful the March of Days

"Forest Green"
Traditional English Melody
Arranged by Ralph Vaughan Williams
Words by Frances W. Wile

1. All beau - ti - ful the march __ of __ days,
2. O'er white ex - pan - ses spark - ling __ pure
3. O thou from whose un - fath - omed __ law

As sea - sons __ come and go;
The ra - diant __ morns un - fold;
The year in __ beau - ty flows,

The hand that shaped the rose __ hath __ wrought
The sol - emn splen - dors of __ the __ night
Thy - self the vi - sion pass - ing __ by

The crys - tal __ of the snow,
Burn bright - er __ through the cold.
In crys - tal __ and in rose,

Hath __ sent the hoar - y __ frost __ of __ heaven,
Life __ mounts in ev - ery __ throb - bing __ vein,
Day __ un - to day __ doth __ ut - ter __ speech,

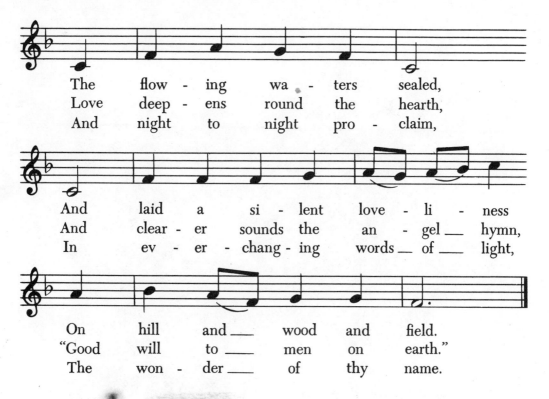

The flow - ing wa - ters sealed,
Love deep - ens round the hearth,
And night to night pro - claim,

And laid a si - lent love - li - ness
And clear - er sounds the an - gel — hymn,
In ev - er - chang - ing words — of — light,

On hill and — wood and field.
"Good will to — men on earth."
The won - der — of thy name.

Lo, the Winter Is Past

Music by Walter Ihrke
Words from the "Song of Solomon"

Very smoothly

For, lo, the win - ter is past; the rain is ___

o - ver and gone. The flow - ers ap - pear on the earth; the

time of the sing - ing of birds is come. _____

More Visual
Art
to Explore

Cave Paintings, c. 15,000-9,000 B.C.
Ralph Morse, LIFE Magazine, © Time Inc.

Jeunes filles au piano, Auguste Renoir (1841-1919, France) Oil on canvas.
Courtesy of the Robert Lehman Collection, New York.

More Visual Art to Explore

Looking at art will help you to understand life in different places and times. It often will express something you have experienced. It will help you imagine experiences you never have had.

In your book you will discover many types of art. There are paintings made with oil paint, watercolor, and chalk. There are drawings and sculptures. There are book illustrations and photographs. Find examples of each type. Talk about the time and place of each example.

Look for the different materials and methods the artist used. Notice the special style of each artist. Create some art products of your own as you explore subjects and methods of expression.

Discuss the differences in painting with oil paint, watercolor, and chalk. Notice how Van Gogh used oil paint in this painting. How can you tell that the artist understood his materials? How did he use imagination? How does the work reflect the time and place in which Van Gogh lived? What else does the painting tell about the artist?

Look at another landscape painting on page 28. What different method of painting and use of imagination do you find?

Cypresses, 1889, Vincent Van Gogh (1853-1890, Holland, France). Oil on canvas, 36¾" x 29⅛".
Metropolitan Museum of Art, New York. Rogers Fund, 1949.

Interior with a Girl Drawing, 1935, Pablo Picasso (1881-   , Spain,
France) Oil.
Private Collection, New York.

In this painting by an artist of our time, notice the people. The
artist did not copy reality but instead used shapes and features
in his own special way. What do these representations tell us that
copies of reality would not tell? Notice the use of colors. Locate
all the green, blue, red, gold, and black areas. Think about why
each color is used where it is. On page iv notice a different style
Picasso used to represent people, and a different color plan. Look
at the painting by another modern artist on page 118 of your
book. Describe his style of representing people. What is his plan
of using colors?

Saint George and the Dragon, Raphael (1483-1520, Italy) Oil.
National Gallery of Art, Washington, D.C. Andrew Mellon Collection.

Many works of art tell a story. Read about St. George and the dragon or listen to your teacher tell the story. Sing the ballad "Sir Eglamore" on page 94, which is a story in music. What other stories can you find in art and in music?

Study of Horses (recto),
Eugène Delacroix
(1798-1863, France) Pen
and wash on cream paper.
The University of Michigan
Museum of Art, Ann Arbor,
Michigan.

On these pages you see horses represented by a painter of long
ago and a painter of recent times. Study each style. Can you
develop your own style of representing animals and birds in
some material you choose?

Three Red Horses, Franz Marc (1880-1916, Germany)
Collection, Paul E. Geier, Rome.

Compare this oil painting with the pastel made with chalk on page 150. The same subject is used by the same artist. Why are the works so different?

Le foyer de la danse, Edgar Degas (1834-1917, France) Oil on canvas. The Louvre, Paris.

You are studying music from Far Away, of Long Ago, and Here and Now. In your book you can see works of art in each category. Locate these and study the special character of each place and time.

Bahram Gur in the Turquoise Palace on Wednesday, 16th Century. Persian miniature: Herat School: Nizami: Khamsa. Detail from folio 224b.
The Metropolitan Museum of Art. Gift of Alexander Smith Cochran, 1913.

Rouen Cathedral, Claude Monet (1840-1926, France) Oil
on canvas.
The Metropolitan Museum of Art. The Theodore M. Davis
Collection. Bequest of Theodore M. Davis, 1915.

Compare this painting of Rouen Cathedral with the photograph
on page 37. How are they different?

Many works of art express subjects related to worship. What story does this painting tell? What music do you know that has to do with worship?

The Journey of the Magi, c. 1430, Stefano di Giovanni Sassetta (1392?-1450) Tempera on panel.
The Metropolitan Museum of Art, New York. Bequest of Maitland F. Griggs, 1943.

Twittering Machine, 1922, Paul Klee (1879-1940, Switzerland) Watercolor, pen and ink, 16¼″ x 12″. Collection: The Museum of Modern Art, New York. Purchase.

A Clown, Honoré Daumier (1808-1879, France) Drawing, charcoal and watercolor. The Metropolitan Museum of Art, New York. Rogers Fund, 1927.

Many times you compose music of your own. Can you create visual arts? Use paints or crayons with paper. Carve in wood, soap, or stone, or create sculpture with paper or metal. What subject will you choose? What materials will be best? Experiment with ideas. Develop a work you are proud of.

Dominant Curve, No. 631, 1936, Vasily Kandinsky (1866-1944, Russia, Germany) Oil on canvas.
The Solomon R. Guggenheim
Museum Collection, New York.

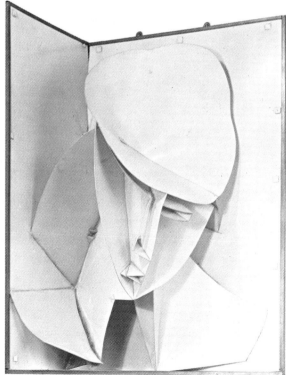

Head of a Woman, c. 1917-1920,
after a work of 1916, Naum Gabo
(1890-   , Russia, Germany,
United States) Construction in
celluloid and metal, 24½″ x 19¼″.
Collection: The Museum of Modern Art,
New York. Purchase.

Spring, 1947, Ben Shahn (1898-1969, Lithuania, United States) Oil.
Albright-Knox Art Gallery, Buffalo, New York.

The works on these pages are on subjects of nature. Looking at
art may help you notice beauties of nature. What other visual
works in your book express something about nature? What music
do you know that has to do with nature?

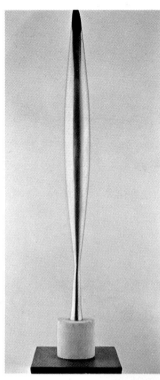

Bird in Space, 1927?,
Constantin Brancusi (1876-1957, Rumania, France)
Bronze, unique cast, 54″ high.
Collection: The Museum of Modern Art, New York.

Landscape with Bluebirds, 1919, Paul Klee (1879-1940, Switzerland) Gouache.
Philadelphia Museum of Art. A. E. Gallatin Collection.

The Vault of Heaven, Detail, 17th Century. Painted
ceiling from Italy.

Classified Index

American Folk Songs and Spirituals

Athapascan Indian Bear-Raven Song (*American Indian*), 86
Bound for the Rio Grande, 165
Dakota Hymn, 164
Doney Gal, 138
Hau-Wari (*American Indian*), 85
My Lord, What a Morning, 100
Old Texas, 8
Polly Wolly Doodle, 6
Quapaw Indian Face-Dance Song (*American Indian*), 87
Railroad Corral, The, 103
Riddle Song, The, 97
Rocka My Soul, 4
Rock Island Line, 102
Shanty Boys in the Pine, The, 101
Swing Low, Sweet Chariot, 158
There Was an Old Witch, 186
This Little Light of Mine, 142
This Train, 131
Trouble in Mind, 166
Ua Nani O Nu'uanu (*Hawaiian*), 160
Virginia Reel, 114
We Sing of Golden Mornings, 26

Composed Songs

All Beautiful the March of Days (*arr. by R. Vaughan Williams*), 198
America (*H. Carey*), 23
America for Me (*W. S. Haynie*), 185
America, the Beautiful (*S. A. Ward*), 144
Blacksmith, The (*J. Brahms*), 175
Butterfly, The (*F. Schubert*), 70
Come, Ye Thankful People, Come (*G. J. Elvey*), 188
Crow, The (*I. Stravinsky*), 128
Happiness (*C. Gesner*), 120
How Does My Lady's Garden Grow? (*A. Frackenpohl*), 124
It's a Small World (*R. Sherman*), 24
It's Quiet on the Moon (*R. de Cesare*), 148
Jesus the Christ Is Born (*J. J. Niles*), 194
Lo, the Winter Is Past (*W. Ihrke*), 200
Mister Urian (*L. van Beethoven*), 66

Power and Glory, The (*P. Ochs*), 2
Psalm 100 (*J. Marshall*), 129
Quiet (*M. Reynolds*), 14
Timely Rhyme, A (*J. Moe*), 125
Troubador Song (*C. Muset*), 96
Waltzing Matilda (*M. Cowan*), 180
We Sing of Golden Mornings (*W. Walker*), 26
Yellow Submarine (*J. Lennon—P. McCartney*), 156

Dances and Singing Games

Crested Hen, The, 75
Gustaf's Skoal, 75
Polly Wolly Doodle, 6
Roberts, The, 177
Siva Siva Maia, 77
Stodola Pumpa, 176
Virginia Reel, 114
Weggis Dance, 76

Folk Listening

Mananitas, Las, 141
Music of Africa, 55
    Frekoba
    Jin-Go-Lo-Ba
    Oyin Momo Ado
This Little Light of Mine, 141
Turkey in the Straw, 114

Folk Songs of Other Countries

Africa
Congo Lullaby (*English and African*), 41
Kum Ba Yah, 34
Laboring Song (*Kwaeja no maka-shot, English and African*), 54

Arabia
Tafta Hindy, 136

Argentina
Mariposita, La (*Spanish*), 72

Australia
Kookaburra, 11
Waltzing Matilda, 180

Austria
Cuckoo, The, 63
Yodlers' Carol, The, 190

Canada
Young Voyageur, The, 106

China
Frogs (*Shu Ha Mo, English and Chinese*), 40
Young Monk, The, 44

Czechoslovakia
Cuckoo Carol, 196
Stodola Pumpa, 176
Where Is John? 50

Denmark
Crested Hen, The, 75
Sim Sala Bim, 68

England
All Beautiful the March of Days, 198
Bell Doth Toll, The, 39
Blow the Wind Southerly, 104
Call John the Boatman, 51
Cherries So Ripe, 89
Little Bells of Westminster, 38
Little Fox, 112
Sir Eglamore, 94
To Thee Before the Close of Day, 36
Troubador Song, 96
We Wish You A Merry Christmas, 189
Why Shouldn't My Goose? 88
Wraggle-Taggle Gypsies, The, 92

France
Au clair de la lune (*French*), 46
French Cathedrals (*French*), 147

Germany
Holla-Hi! Holla-Ho! 22
Joseph Dearest, Joseph Mild, 193
Shepherd's Song, The, 10

Greece
Sponge Fishing, 60

Holland
Bezem, De (*Dutch*), 62

India
Hari Krishna (*Indian*), 35

Israel
Brethren in Peace Together (*Jewish Folk Song*), 130
Once, 21
Pretty Little Girl, Can You Answer Me? 178
Zum Gali Gali (*Hebrew*), 137

Alphabetical Index of Music and Poetry